The Parihaka Cult

Kerry Bolton

The Parihaka Cult

Kerry Bolton

ISBN-13: 978-1-910881-68-2

Black House Publishing Ltd
Kemp House
152 City Road
London
UNITED KINGDOM
EC1V 2NX

www.blackhousepublishing.com
Email: info@blackhousepublishing.com

Contents

Contents

Foreword

Over the past forty-years or so, we in New Zealand have watched our history being systematically re-invented, not based upon documented evidence of real-events that actually occurred on the ground, but solely to serve a modern-day need for made-to-order propaganda.

One of the foremost of the churned-out, manufactured-myths surrounds the mid-19th century creation of a cultist-community called 'Parihaka', now represented, in typical Marxist-speak, as some kind of a Gandhi-inspiring bastion of righteousness and (yawn) passive-resistance against imperialist tyranny.

Dr. Kerry Bolton delves deeply into the huge body of extant historical documentation, contemporary to Parihaka's founding prophet, and lays the entire, lame-fantasy bare for all to see. What has been emotively bantered-about as New Zealand's 'Holocaust' or 'Genocide' at Parihaka, due to the very belated intervention by troops of a long-suffering government, renders-down to little more than a Maori boy with a sore foot, after it was trodden on by a horse.

Propagandised New Zealand students in our educational institutions are hereby advised: When history class starts, just go outside and kick a ball around or something; it would be considerably more beneficial!

Martin Doutré

Introduction

Parihaka is a Maori community in the Taranaki district of the North Island of New Zealand. Its name has been made synonymous, along with that of its 'prophet' Te Whiti, with 'passive resistance' to European land settlement and governance during the latter part of the 19th Century. It is described in utopian terms as having been a prosperous model community that the Colonial Government tried to brutally destroy.

The Government occupation of Parihaka in 1881 has assumed the New Zealand equivalent of South Africa's Sharpeville Massacre and the USA's Wounded Knee. The cult of Parihaka, based on the personalities of Te Whiti and his eventual rival Tohu, are analogous to the cults of the Muslim *Mahdi* and of the Ghost Dance manifestation among the Lakota American Indians, at around the same time. Te Whiti is upheld as New Zealand's equivalent to Martin Luther King and Mahatma Ghandi, and is said to be the precursor of these as a great apostle of passive resistance. This book re-examines the nature of the Parihaka cult by going to the sources of the time, comparing these with the present-day versions, and concludes that the events at Parihaka have been distorted in the interests of contemporary political agendas.

Parihaka is already enshrined by national and local government bureaucracies and the education system as an essential part of New Zealand's historical narrative. It is the New Zealand aspect of a worldwide postcolonial political agenda that denigrates the history and identity of Western Civilisation.

3

1 - Post-Colonial Myths

Since the post-World War II era, when the USSR and the USA emerged as the super-powers in a bi-polar world order, the dominant outlook in academia throughout much of the world has been to disparage the European colonial empires, with a concomitant idealisation of ex-colonial peoples. Europe emerged exhausted and indebted in the aftermath of World War II, and the USA and USSR aimed to fill the void, as the European powers were obliged to surrender their empires.[1] Another related agenda has been to glorify the 'national liberation struggles' of 'indigenous peoples', from which, ironically, the supposedly 'anti-imperialist' USA has not been immune. In so doing the revived 'cult of the Noble Savage' has been extended to America's relations with African slaves and American Indians.

Indeed, America's African slave heritage is the basis for scapegoating Caucasians for the ongoing failure of Afro-Americans to successfully integrate into American society. Like Pakeha[2] New Zealand's relations with the Maori, and

---

1   K R Bolton, 'The Geopolitics of White Dispossession'.
2   Pakeha has been the Maori name for White New Zealanders since colonial times. It is often thought to be a derogatory term and numerous meanings have been attached to it. This author accepts the name as most likely derived from Pakepakeha, sea-faring demi-gods with fair skin and hair. They are linked in Maori myth to the Patupaiarehe, a white, blonde or red haired forest-dwelling folk said, according to legend, to have been in New Zealand prior to the Maori. See: Jodie Ranford, 'Pakeha'. Dr Andrew Fraser questions my acceptance of the term even in this relatively positive context, contending that the acceptance seems to reflect acquiescence by British-descended New Zealanders, asking: 'Does that linguistic convention reflect the effective subordination of the once-proudly British identity of New Zealanders to a hegemonic Maori narrative that reduces WASPs to the status of just another ethnic group now isolated from their kith and kin overseas?' Fraser to Bolton, personal correspondence, 1 August 2012. The term Pakeha, I contend, rather might be adapted in a more positive manner to the increasingly popular, albeit heretical, view that Maori legends were correct in regard to Caucasian (urukehu = red haired) peoples settling here prior to the Polynesian arrivals.

the Afrikaners' relations with South African Blacks, there has been much distortion regarding the history of Black slavery in America. Fictionalisations such as the book and television 'docudrama' *Roots* are typical but by no means unique examples.[3] The actual circumstances of Black slavery in America are not as simple as the common assumptions. Contemporary records show that slaves existed in better conditions than Northern white labourers.[4] However such facts do not accord with political agendas. Several of the conclusions drawn by Professors Fogel and Engelman (*liberal* academics, it might be noted) include:

The belief that slave-breeding, sexual exploitation, and promiscuity destroyed the black family is a myth. The family was the basic unit of social organisation under slavery. It was to the economic interests of planters to encourage the stability of slave families and most of them did so....

The material (not psychological) conditions of the lives of slaves compared favourably with those of free industrial workers. This is not to say that they were good by modern standards. It merely emphasized the hard lot of all workers, free or slave, during the first half of the nineteenth century.

Slaves were exploited in the sense that part of the income which they produced was expropriated by their owners. However, the rate of expropriation was much lower than has generally been presumed. Over the course of his lifetime, the typical slave field hand received about 90 percent of the income he produced.[5]

These Caucasian peoples include elements of the Waitaha, and the still extant remnant of the Ngati Hotu in Whanganui. Cf. Doutré, *Ancient Celtic New Zealand*. On the Ngati Hotu see: Raynor Capper, Franklin E-Local. The subject remains for this writer an interesting hypothesis.

3   Alex Haley, Roots.
4   R W Fogel and S L Engerman, Time on the Cross.
5   *Ibid.*, p. 5.

1 - Post-Colonial Myths

The Parihaka myth, like *Roots* and other popular accounts of 'colonialism', has become blurred as to fact and romance. Books such as the novel *The Parihaka Woman* undoubtedly confuse gullible readers who find it difficult to distinguish between fact and fiction; the differences between a work of scholarship and an 'historical novel' or 'docudrama'. Hence, *The Parihaka Woman* is described as 'weaving together fact and fiction', and the gullible reader unconsciously assimilates what has been read without drawing distinctions between the two:

> There has never been a New Zealand novel quite like *The Parihaka Woman*. Richly imaginative and original, weaving together fact and fiction, it sets the remarkable story of Erenora against the historical background of the turbulent and compelling events that occurred in Parihaka during the 1870s and 1880s. Parihaka is the place Erenora calls home, a peaceful Taranaki settlement overcome by war and land confiscation.[6]

The Parihaka myth as part of a worldwide offensive to denigrate The Western heritage and to exaggerate or invent the achievements of others,[7] shares analogous features with the Wounded Knee myth in the USA. Here we see Wovoka, like Te Whiti and Tohu, supposedly a prophet, agitating the Lakota, stating that Jesus had returned in the form of a Native American.

---

6   Wheelers, The Parihaka Woman, 'Description'.
7   Cf. Basil Davidson, whose book Old Africa Rediscovered was one of the first of our era to ascribe great civilisations and empires to Sub-Saharan Africans, whose achievements had been forgotten due to the racial arrogance of white colonial oppressors. Nonetheless, even Davidson shows that what there was of the accoutrements of civilisation are ascribable to the influences of ancient Egyptians, Arabs, and Chinese. Like subsequent postmodernists, Davidson finds it necessary, in inventing a history for Sub-Saharan Africa, to also belittle Europeans. Hence, Davidson states, for example, that 'the African coastal cities were as civilised as most of the maritime cities of Europe; more civilised than some of them', and describes the Portuguese as 'the natives of a rather backward European country'. Davidson, p. 232. Such pre-postmodernist historical deconstruction has attained significance, becoming a major part of the educational system, exemplified in the USA, for example, with 'Black History Month', when children are taught that Cleopatra and Hannibal were Black Africans.

Like the Maori Hau Hau cult and the Mahdi cult in 19th Century Sudan, Wovoka claimed that his followers would be impervious to bullets.[8] He prophesied a version of the 'Rapture' of American Indians, after which the white man would be eliminated from America. The Ghost Dance invented by Wovoka became a widespread ceremony to fulfil his prophecies.

In December 1890, as the 7th Cavalry attempted to disarm the Lakota people, a Medicine Man, Yellow Bird, started performing the Ghost Dance to remind his people that they were bullet-proof. When a struggle ensued to disarm one of the Lakota, Yellow Bird exhorted warriors to resist, as they could not be killed. On a signal Lakota warriors brought forth concealed weapons and began to fire.[9] Other Lakota had also been armed and ready. The ensuing chaotic, close quarters gun fight caused deaths on both sides, but this is portrayed as a great injustice to the Lakota and is memorialised today in a way paralleling that of Parihaka. Despite there apparently having been a plan by at least a faction of the Lakota to open fire on the military at the signal of Yellow Bird, who clearly wanted to contrive a violent confrontation, like Te Whiti, the blame for the conflict is placed entirely with the cavalry, just as Bryce, who led the occupation of Parihaka, has ever since been ridiculed and castigated.

Like the legend of Parihaka as it has come down to the present, the Ghost Dance cult and the confrontation at Wounded Knee are presented as a misunderstanding as to the character of the cult by the authorities. The same laudatory perceptions of Te Whiti and Parihaka are maintained by writers such as Riseborough and Winder, and given sanction as the 'party line' by New Zealand national and local government bodies. Likewise, Wounded Knee has become a rallying cry for political agitation, culminating in a violent confrontation between radicals of the American Indian Movement and US Marshals at Wounded Knee in 1973.[10]

8   'Mahdi', Encyclopedia of the Middle East.
9   R M Utley, p. 210.
10   US Marshal's Service, 'Wounded Knee'.

8

1 - Post-Colonial Myths

The alleged 'extermination' of Tasmania's Australian Aborigines by settlers is another of the postcolonial versions of history the accuracy of which has also been uncritically assumed. Australian scholar Keith Windshuttle eventually challenged the claim. Windshuttle pointed out that this supposed 'genocide' comprised the deaths of 118 Tasmanian Aborigines[11] out of a total population of 2000 at the time of colonial settlement. In comparison, 187 white settlers had been killed[12] in skirmishes with the Aborigines. However, the supposed 'genocidal policy' against the Tasmanian 'Blackfellows' has become a major part of postcolonialism, and Windshuttle was predictably damned for his heresy by the liberal intelligentsia.

The Sharpeville Massacre of 21 March 1960 can be placed in the same category of post-colonial mythologizing. The irony is that the target community, the Afrikaners, were themselves subjects of the British Empire. They fought a war against the British that included the incarceration of their women and children into British concentration camps where over 26,000 died of typhus,[13] a fact that does not seem to merit attention from those who are eager to portray the Afrikaners as colonial oppressors.[14]

The Sharpeville Massacre is popularly described as the shooting of sixty-nine peaceful Black demonstrators protesting the Pass Laws, the very laws that had been designed to protect jobs for indigenous Blacks from illegal immigrants, and to maintain orderly migrations of labour. The 'pass laws' nonetheless became a *cause celebre* against apartheid. Thousands of demonstrators organised by the African National Congress (ANC) and the Pan Africanist Congress (PAC) surrounded the police station at Sharpeville.[15] Several months previously (January) nine policemen (four white and five Zulu) had been stoned and

---

11 K Windshuttle, 2002, Vol. I, p. 397.
12 *Ibid.*, p. 352.
13 T Pakenham, The Boer War, p. 607.
14 T B Floyd, passim.
15 Ramon Lewis Leigh, Vereeniging History, Turmoil at Sharpeville, p. 58. http://www.vaaltriangleinfo.co.za/history/vereeniging/chapter_15/58.htm

hacked to death by drunken partygoers when they were on a routine patrol in Cato Manor, Durban.[16]

The Sharpeville rioters cut telegraph lines to isolate the police station, and armed with poles and *pangas* (homemade machetes), the preferred weapon of the PAC, and throwing rocks, converged on a line of police.[17] Demonstrators elsewhere had been dispersed, mainly peacefully, but low flying jets had failed to have effect at Sharpeville. The PAC officials had presented themselves inside the police station, demanding that they be arrested for breaking the 'pass laws', but the police had refused to respond to these attempts to cause confrontation. As an alternative to being hacked and stoned to death, the police opened fire. Since the PAC had cut the phone lines, emergency services were slow to arrive to tend to casualties.

While the world's media fell in behind the party-line and portrayed the PAC directed savagery as state violence against unarmed Black protestors, Dr Heinrich Verwoerd, Prime Minister, gave some background to the events soon after:

> At Sharpeville, Colonel Pienaar, in command of the police there, had to force his way through a crowd of about 20,000 Bantu who had surrounded the police station. ...Stones rained on the police and the mob advanced on them. Colonel Pienaar then gave orders for the police to load. At that moment three shots were fired at the police from within the Bantu crowd. The shouting crowd advanced and the police fired a volley with Sten guns and 303s without an order having been given to fire. ...He regretted that the effect of all the propaganda of the past years had brought the government's handling of Bantu affairs under suspicion and these people had now been instigated to try

---

16   Turmoil at Sharpville, p. 59. http://www.vaaltriangleinfo.co.za/history/vereeniging/
      chapter_15/59.htm
17   Reports normally claim the rioters were 'unarmed', and the stone throwing incidents
      are denied, although photographs show that stones had been thrown.

the impossible and challenge the authority of the state.[18]

As in the examples of Parihaka and the riots instigated everywhere that Martin Luther King spoke, the 'Sharpeville Massacre' had been preceded by cynical claims by ANC and PAC leaders that the demonstrations would be 'peaceful'. Immediately after the Sharpeville riot, there were Black rampages in which other Blacks who had worked instead of observing a 'Day of Mourning', were viciously attacked by the ANC and PAC mobs, and public buildings – especially schools and churches, were set afire. While it can – or should - now be more clearly seen how savage the ANC and other 'anti-apartheid' movements were, the myth continues in maintaining the saintly image against the evil Afrikaners, and praises are sung to high heaven on the 'Rainbow Nation' while nothing is said about the murder of Afrikaner farmers and the shambolic character of post-apartheid South Africa under the godly visage of Nelson Mandela.

21st March is officially designated Human Rights Day in South Africa in honour of the rioters. Sharpeville is heralded as an example of 'passive resistance'.[19] Yet, the PAC, according to a PAC speech appended by Gerhart and Glaser[20] upholds Sharpeville as the beginning of 'armed resistance', and a manoeuvre that had been carefully planned by this breakaway faction of the ANC.

There is a common mentality and agenda that upholds these myths of postcolonialism across the world. Parihaka is the New Zealand example. The propaganda is given a scholarly façade under the name of 'postmodernism'.

---

18   'Verwoerd Gives Riot Details', Cape Times.
19   An account of the Sharpeville riot and background events can be found at: Why We Are White Refugees, 'The Road to Sharpeville and the ANC's Orwellian Memoryhole', http://why-we-are-white-refugees.blogspot.com/2010/03/road-to-sharpeville-and-ancs-orwellian.html
     Depicted are press photographs of stockpiles of weapons that had been carried by the 'peaceful, unarmed' rioters.
20   Gerhart and Glaser, p.557.

The Character of 'Passive Resistance'

Te Whiti has been upheld as a pioneer of 'passive resistance' and a precursor of Martin Luther King. Indeed, one can expect a push to have a 'Te Whiti Day' commemorated in the manner of 'Martin Luther King Day' in the USA. Passive resistance is a strategy of tension. It is designed to oblige state authorities to use force to maintain order. It can then be claimed that the state was undertaking aggression against peace protestors.

That such 'passive resistance' is designed not merely to highlight a cause, but to cause a confrontation is not usually recognised. Therefore when Martin Luther King flooded Blacks, and a goodly number of Whites and Jews from the North, into the Southern states, his aim was to create disruption and force the authorities to take action in the only manner they could – physically. When appeals to disperse are unheeded, there is no other option. Likewise, when Te Whiti moved hundreds of his followers onto a white farm, and the authorities were obliged to remove them – albeit in a lenient manner, and at times without even arrest – the myth was enabled that Te Whiti and his followers were the peaceful victims of colonial oppression.

In particular, a notable, and cynical strategy of such 'passive resistance' is the use of women and children in the frontlines of protest. Te Whiti was adept at the use of this tactic, even forming children into special contingents, as we shall see.

Martin Luther King, in his condemnation of 'moderates', described the strategy in his famous 'Letter from a Birmingham Jail:

> Nonviolent direct action seeks to create such a crisis and foster such a tension that a community which has constantly refused to negotiate is forced to confront the issue. It seeks so to dramatize the issue that it can no longer be ignored. My citing the creation of tension as part of the work of the nonviolent resister may sound rather shocking. But I

must confess that I am not afraid of the word 'tension'. I have earnestly opposed violent tension, but there is a type of constructive, nonviolent tension which is necessary for growth... The purpose of our direct action program is to create a situation so crisis packed that it will inevitably open the door to negotiation. [21]

Like Te Whiti with his 'metaphors', King talked of 'nonviolent tension' and fostering 'crisis'. King even disparaged the lenient manner that Southern police dealt with the public disorder he caused, as such leniency did not serve the strategy of tension and crisis.[22] Te Whiti and his followers maintained the same attitude, and would become highly irritated if the Constabulary did not arrest them.

This type of 'passive resistance' that is intended to force a physical reaction from the state authorities, in order to claim martyr status, is moral humbug; it is hypocrisy. It is analogous to the riots against the Springbok rugby tour of New Zealand in 1981 when police confronted thousands of helmeted demonstrators who were carrying shields, and where gang members were put at the front lines. The necessity of police to establish public order against demonstrators running riot has become part of the New Zealand postmodern narrative that has supposedly 'defined who we are'. The supposedly idyllic existence of today's post-apartheid South Africa, 'the Rainbow Nation', is apparently sufficient justification for the riots, just as are the apparently wonderful gains made by Afro-Americans as the result of King's riots to desegregate the South. Now Afro-American children have the freedom to violently run amok in the hallways and classrooms of desegregated schools, making teaching impossible, and the Bantu have the freedom to kill Boer farmers and turn a once prosperous nation into yet another African basket case – under the benevolent smile of Saint Nelson.

---

21   M L King, 1963.
22   *Ibid.*

Postcolonial Studies

The party-line in academia that sees the pre- and post-colonial peoples as sacrosanct has been rendered as a new branch of social science called 'post-colonial studies'. This is based on the sanctification of ex-colonial peoples (other than the white Afrikaners, of course). Like much else in contemporary society, this is heralded as 'progressive' and 'modern' thinking, yet it is a reversion to theories that emerged in the 18th century, as part of a political agenda, which had a romantic notion of colonial peoples as 'noble savages', uncorrupted by 'civilisation'. This was based on ideological assumptions rather than empirical evidence, as the theorists of this doctrine lacked experience with the exotic regions in which such peoples were supposed to exist in such a tranquil state.

In its introduction to 'post-colonial studies' as part of English Literature, Emory University offers some definitions of what is a typically open-ended condemnation of European peoples:

> The field of Postcolonial Studies has been gaining prominence since the 1970s. Some would date its rise in the Western academy from the publication of Edward Said's influential critique of Western constructions of the Orient in his 1978 book, *Orientalism*. The growing currency within the academy of the term 'postcolonial' (sometimes hyphenated) was consolidated by the appearance in 1989 of *The Empire Writes Back: Theory and Practice in Post-Colonial Literatures* by Bill Ashcroft, Gareth Griffiths, and Helen Tiffin. Although there is considerable debate over the precise parameters of the field and the definition of the term 'postcolonial', in a very general sense, it is the study of the interactions between European nations and the societies they colonized in the modern period.[23]

It is apparent that 'post-colonial studies' is intended as part

23   Emory University, 'Introduction to Postcolonial Studies'.

of a broad front for the theoretical deconstruction of Western Civilisation, and is part and parcel of a neo-Marxian movement in academia that includes such burgeoning 'disciplines' (?) as 'gender studies'. Emory University's introduction continues:

> Despite the reservations and debates, research in Postcolonial Studies is growing because postcolonial critique allows for a wide-ranging investigation into power relations in various contexts. The formation of empire, the impact of colonization on postcolonial history, economy, science, and culture, the cultural productions of colonized societies, feminism and postcolonialism, agency for marginalized people, and the state of the postcolony in contemporary economic and cultural contexts are some broad topics in the field.[24]

The book *Quest for Origins* by Dr Kerry Howe[25] is one such example of 'postcolonial studies', written as an attempt to disprove unorthodox, but increasingly popular, theories on the ancient settlement of New Zealand. Howe sets out to demolish, often with a dose of *ad hominem*, the unconventional views of researchers such as Martin Doutré,[26] Thor Heyerdahl,[27] Dr Barry Fell,[28] Barry Brailsford,[29] et al. who have suggested that races other than 'Maori' reached New Zealand in antiquity.[30]

Howe refers to his methodology as 'postmodern and postcolonial' 'deconstruction', and as an 'intellectual revolution' in academia. This deconstruction is a revision of past historical views to accord

---

24 *Ibid.*
25 Howe is Professor of History at Massey University, Albany Campus, Auckland, New Zealand.
26 M Doutré, 1999. Oddly, Howe in his 'Bibliography' gives the date of publication of Doutré's book Ancient Celtic New Zealand as 'c. 2000' (Howe, p. 212) although the publication date is clearly stated on the book as 1999 (Doutré, p. 1), which suggests that Howe might not have actually read the book.
27 T Heyerdahl, 1952.
28 B Fell, 1975.
29 B Brailsford, 1994.
30 K Howe, pp. 139-158.

with the postmodern world. Howe states that this method asks not 'what happened and why' but 'how has history been constructed and thus who is it for? All knowledge is now revealed to have political positioning, and to be relative. There is no fixed, value-free observation post'. 'Reality' and 'truth' are relative according to the perspectives of their observers.[31] *We can, then, just as well ask: who is this 'postmodern' theory of history for and how is it being constructed?* Windshuttle similarly described the same process of 'postmodernism', but is critical of the way historical research is moulded to serve political agendas:

> In the last few decades, all of this — the entire intellectual heritage of history writing — has come under challenge within our universities. Academic historians have argued that the attempt to distance themselves from their own political system cannot be done. According to many, history is "inescapably political". In tandem with this has come the notion that history cannot be objective because there are no independent vantage points from which one can look down on the past... Under this notion, different cultures and even different political positions each have their own truths, even if they are incompatible with the truths of other cultures. This stance generally goes under the name of postmodernism....
>
> Overall, then, in the writing and teaching of history today, the views that are in the ascendancy are those that support a skepticism about the pursuit of objectivity and truth, and those that want to replace political and military history and their focus on great men, with social history and its focus on minority or disadvantaged groups.[32]

Windhshuttle cites a document describing the purpose of the National Museum of Australia, when it opened in 2001:

---

31   *Ibid.*, p. 16.
32   K Windshuttle, 2007.

The impact of postmodernism has meant that ... triumphalist stories of national progress are no longer intellectually tenable. Many museum practitioners now see their work as a critical practice, committed to drawing out the ways in which constructions of race, class and gender (and sometimes sexuality and age) have shaped national histories

Windshuttle commented on the Museum's declaration of purpose:

The result is that most of the people celebrated in the museum's exhibits are those who fit within the categories of 'interest group' politics, that is, the politics of feminism, gay liberation, radical environmentalism, and the politics of Aborigines and ethnic groups. The white males who established Australia's political, legal and educational institutions and those who played major roles in building our economy barely rate a mention.[33]

Hence, we see from two opposing opinions, Windshuttle and Howe, that 'postcolonialism' and 'postmodernism' are intended to serve political agendas rather than the 'truth' *per se*. 'Facts' become relative in the service of political agendas. The attitude of much of present Western academia is analogous to that of the USSR whose sciences were subjected to ideological conformity. One particularly ridiculous example was the replacing of Mendelian genetics with the neo-Lamarckian doctrines of Lysenko, who almost brought Soviet agriculture to ruin before he was banished – albeit after several decades of holding sway - back to obscurity.[34] Genetics, even when applied to agronomy, was regarded as inherently 'fascist' and anti-Marxist. In the meantime, those scientists who sought to defend genetics were regarded as enemies of the state. They were removed from their positions.

33   *Ibid.*
34   Z A Medvedev, passim

Is the present-day situation in 'postmodern' Western academia any freer than it was in the USSR? Dr Andrew Fraser commented on his observations and experiences in Australia: 'If my experience as a teacher, scholar, and, more recently, a first-year theology student is a reliable guide, academia is utterly hostile to free thought and frank discussion on race, ethnicity, and gender'.[35] Dr Fraser was summarily suspended from Macquarie University in 2005 for having critiqued African immigration. His scholarly paper, 'Rethinking the White Australia Policy' was then barred from *Deakin Law Review*, published by Deakin University.[36]

Where this dogmatism leads in New Zealand can be seen in the condemnation and ridicule of Dr Greg Clydesdale of Massey University,[37] when in 2008 he was declared heretical by Members of Parliament, news media, the Race Relations Conciliator, academia, et al for having written a paper[38] that documented the blatantly obvious: Polynesians are an economic underclass in an economy whose manufacturing base has long since been wrecked. Pointing out with statistical data the continuing underachievement of Polynesians educationally and professionally is analogous to the boy who cried out 'the emperor has no clothes'. Yet, the head of the 'Pasifika' department, Sione Tu'itahi, at Clydesdale's own university castigated his colleague, the banal reaction being featured on Massey's website lest the University be mistaken as having endorsed empirical evidence rather than emotion-laden dogma on such matters. Furthermore, the University demonstrated its malice against Dr Clydesdale, commenting: 'Massey University has welcomed the announcement by Race Relations Conciliator Joris de Bres that he will investigate Dr Clydesdale's report. It is expected that several Massey academics and other staff will be pleased to participate in any review'.[39] Dr Clydesdale was

35   A Fraser, 'The Cult of "The Other"'.
36   *Ibid.*
37   Clydesdale is with the faculty of Management and Business at Massey University, Palmerston North, New Zealand.
38   G Clydesdale, 2008.
39   'Massey's Pasifika', Massey University, 2008.

obliged to forego the presentation of his paper to an academic conference in Brazil on economic development: New Zealand's false image as a multicultural utopia could not be exposed to the outside world, any more than negative aspects of life behind the Iron Curtain could be exposed to outside scrutiny.

Hence, we might see that such postcolonial legends as Sharpeville, Wounded Knee and Parihaka are subject to re-rendering by academia from the perspective of postcolonial and postmodern political agendas.

The newspaper and other accounts of the time in regard to Parihaka, as referenced in this book, for example, can therefore be conveniently dismissed as nothing more than the value-judgements of colonialists, rather than as accurate eye-witness accounts of events as they took place. Thereby, history can be deconstructed and reconstructed according to political agendas.

Hereditary Collective Guilt

The tendency is for the European peoples, or rather governments in their name, to forever apologise for the alleged wrongdoings of the colonial era. This universal guilt complex is transposed to the present so that reparations can be demanded in perpetuity on the basis of *collective and hereditary guilt*. Hence, European peoples will be forever judged 'guilty' for the alleged 'crimes' of their 'colonial oppressor' forebears.

In New Zealand, this collective and hereditary guilt is accompanied by continual apologies for the supposed wrongs of our pioneers, and has become an integral part in the implementation of the 'Treaty of Waitangi'. It is enshrined in the laws of New Zealand, as part of a postcolonial process of formulating new 'Treaty principles' that are far beyond what was originally envisaged by the signatories of the Treaty over 170 years ago. [40]

---

40   D Round, passim.

The abject manner by which European peoples are expected to conduct themselves towards ex-colonial subjects'[41] in the postcolonial era have reached the proportions of sick farce. Now there are demands for the British Government to apologise to Mau Mau veterans for alleged 'mistreatment' as prisoners during their bestial terrorist insurgency in Kenya during the 1950s.[42] That paragon of humanity, Archbishop Desmond Tutu, has urged the British to concede to the Mau Mau veterans.[43] Such native antics would not even have been imagined had they not been prompted by the postcolonial renderings of history by British academics.

Like Parihaka, Sharpeville and Wounded Knee, the Mau Mau uprising becomes a part of the postcolonial narrative that places guilt entirely upon Europeans. Hence, a book that accuses the *British* of atrocities against the Mau Mau was awarded a Pulitzer Prize in 2006.[44] Caroline Elkins of Harvard University, author of *Imperial Reckoning*, ascribes a genocidal plot against the Kikuyu to the British: 'I now believe there was in late colonial Kenya a murderous campaign to eliminate Kikuyu people that left tens of thousands, perhaps hundreds of thousands dead'.[45] Thus, even the Mau Mau in the postcolonial dispensation are vested with a saintly aura, because anything is justified in vilifying the European.

The Myth of the 'Noble Savage'

Just how 'modern' such 'post-colonial scholarship' is can be seen from its origins in a novel published in 1688, *Oroonoko*, by Aphra Behn. Set in Surinam, South America, it is the story of two royal slaves, Oroonoko, an African prince, and his beloved Imoinda. This short novel seems to have been the first to have presented the image of the 'noble savage'. In 1701 John Dryden

---

41   Not, however, including White ex-colonial subjects such as the Afrikaners.
42   'Mau Mau Oaths'.
43   Daily Mail, 'Mau Mau Trio...'
44   Pulitzer Prizes, 2006.
45   C Elkins, Imperial Reckoning.

was expressing the sentiment poetically in 'The Conquest of Granada':

I am free as nature first made man,
Ere the base laws of servitude began.
When wild in the woods the noble savage ran.

However it was several decades later that Jean Jacques Rousseau presented the myth of the 'noble savage' as the basis of a philosophical system that provided the foundation for both liberal and communist ideologies. Such philosophising laid the groundwork for the French Revolution of 1789, which was intended to return humanity to a theoretical utopia. However, like all such utopian visions – including the Communism of our own era - when theory does not accord with practice, the resort is to the guillotine, mass murder,[46] and the more sophisticated means of extermination of our own times. While the postmodernist academics – like their Communist predecessors – continually remind the world of the horrors supposedly attendant with 'fascism', a term that has been expanded to encompass virtually any non-Left movement, Jacobin France, with its 'Reign of Terror' and the outright genocide of the Vendée' French, is seldom recalled as the predecessor not only of Communism but also of Liberalism, the foundation of postmodernist doctrine. Hence, as we will consider briefly below, recourse to suppression of free enquiry and free speech, when these threaten certain cherished dogmas of Liberal-democracy, is a feature of the present postmodern era.

Rousseau wrote in his seminal *Discourse of the Origin of the Inequality Among Men*: 'Man in his natural state was born essentially good and free of all prejudices', and becomes corrupted through civilisational institutions such as private property and marriage. However, at least Rousseau conceded that his doctrine was speculative rather than the result of empirical observation.

---

46 The Vendée region of France, for example, was devastated and depopulated by the Jacobin regime due to its stubborn loyalty to Catholicism. See: Sophie Masson, 'Remembering the Vendée'.

The discovery of the South Sea Islanders seemed to confirm the theories of Europe's drawing room intelligentsia, romantic novelists and poets. Philip Commerson, naturalist on the expedition under Louis-Anotonie Bougainville, wrote in *Mercure de France* that he had observed this Rousseauan state of bliss amongst the islanders where, 'the state of natural man, born essentially good, free from all preconceptions and following without suspicion and without remorse the gentle impulse of an instinct that is always sure because it has not yet degenerated into reason'. Bougainville, having visited Tahiti for less than two weeks, waxed lyrical: 'Everywhere we went we found hospitality, peace, innocence and joy and every appearance of happiness'.[47]

Conflict between empirical anthropological research and dogmatic beliefs serving political ends became apparent in 1984, when Australian anthropologist Dr Derek Freeman wrote a refutation of the seminal work of venerated American anthropologist Margaret Mead's *Coming of Age in Samoa* (1928). Freeman, emeritus professor of anthropology at Australian National University, Foundation Professor of Anthropology at the University of Samoa, and an honorary Samoan chief who knows the society intimately, was met with outrage when he showed that Mead's research methodology and conclusions on Samoan life were flawed. Like the 17th and 18th century romantic novelists and drawing room theorists, Mead had sought to give legitimacy to the notion of the 'Noble Savage' by writing that Samoan adolescents had none of the problems of Western youth, and that Samoa was an inherently peaceful society. Freeman showed that Mead had been incorrect on all levels, and that Samoan society since before colonial contact, had been violence ridden and far from idyllic.[48]

Mead's *Coming of Age* was a pioneer of postcolonial theory. She was in turn mentored by the father of American cultural

---

47   Bougainville, 1771, Quoted by D S Garden, p. 142.
48   D Freeman, passim.

anthropology, Professor Franz Boas of Columbia University, whose coterie of students came to dominate anthropology not only in the USA but throughout the West. Boasian anthropology is based on the primacy of the environment on culture and society, and the repudiation of any genetic foundations. Boasian cultural anthropology and the predominant thinking in sociology are the Western equivalents to the USSR's Lysenkoism, a difference being that the USSR eventually repudiated Lysenko,[49] whereas Boasianism is still entrenched in the Western social sciences. Freeman describes the Boasian origins and influences at length in his book on Mead.[50] Boas was a Marxist with Communist sympathies, and his theories accord with Communist doctrine.[51] Hence they found ready support among Leftist and liberal academia and continue to do so.

It is notable that the subtitle of Mead's book, which was introduced by her mentor, Franz Boas, is 'A Psychological Study of Primitive Youth for Western Civilisation'.[52] The lesson to be adopted by the Westerner is that his civilisation is lacking the carefree spirit of the primitive. The answer to our social maladies is to learn from the 'Noble Savage'.

In the New Zealand context the Maori continues to be portrayed as having a society that was in pre-colonial times morally and socially superior to the Western; more nurturing, and more family oriented. Most of all, traditional Maori society was attuned to the environment, which has been ravished by the greedy Pakeha. Again, the image is based on postcolonial agendas. Davidson summarises the situation:

> Today there is a tendency to be highly critical of European colonisation of the land while praising the pre-European Maoris as conservationists who treated New Zealand with

---

49 Z A Medvedev, op. cit.
50 D Freeman, op. cit., pp. 18-61.
51 G Bullert, pp. 208-243.
52 M Mead, op. cit.

care and respect. While there is no doubt the Maoris did have a great affinity and love of the land, there is equally no doubt that they did substantially and irreversibly alter the pre-European landscape.[53]

The Polynesians in pre-colonial times caused widespread environmental damage throughout the entire region. Mitchell stated that prior to European settlement, throughout the Pacific Islands Polynesians felled coastal forests, with the damage expanding inland and into the valleys.[54] The forests were burnt, imported weeds flourished, resulting erosion destroyed fertile land. Mitchell described the results of Polynesian disforestation as 'disastrous', and as destroying resources. In Hawaii Polynesians 'extinguished perhaps forty species of bird' prior to European colonisation. Mitchell adds that 'these discoveries have not gone down well with native Hawaiians anxious to maintain the myth of Polynesians as guardians of Paradise'.[55] The situation in New Zealand with the arrival of the Maori parallels that of the other Polynesian islands. Archaeologist Bruce McFadgen writes that with the coming of the Maori 'almost half of the forest was burnt off, all twelve species of moa became extinct, at least twenty other bird species became extinct, tuatara and other birds and animals became extinct in certain areas, seals and other sea mammals, which had previously bred all around the coastline, were reduced to breeding in only a few locations'.[56] However, such facts are not permitted to interfere with the popularised notion of Maori as the 'tangata whenua' ('the people of the land')[57] who are custodians attempting to hold out against Pakeha exploitation.

The urge to romanticise the 'exotic' in contrast to what one

---

53   J Davidson, 1984.
54   A Mitchell, 1989.
55   *Ibid.*
56   B McFadgen, 1987.
57   'Tangata whenua: local people, hosts, indigenous people of the land - people born of the whenua, i.e. of the placenta and of the land where the people's ancestors have lived and where their placenta are buried'. *Maori Dictionary.*

might perceive as the shortcomings of one's own society, is far older than even that of Behn's 17ᵗʰ century novel. One might see an analogy in the idolisation of the Germanics by Tacitus writing in the first century A.D. in contrasting what he regarded as the decadence of Roman society. However, with the doctrine of the 'Noble Savage' as it has come down to us today, we find a dogma presently enshrined by the intelligentsia just as much as in the times of 18ᵗʰ century European revolutionary ferment. The Parihaka myth is within that ideological mould.

II - The Making of the Parihaka Myth

While New Zealanders have long been taught that the European settlers held the Maori in universal contempt as a savage enemy, and cheated him out of his lands, this was far from the case, as newspaper accounts of the time show. Maori even then enjoyed much sympathy from all sectors of the European population, both 'high' and 'low', and Te Whiti especially often received favourable treatment from sections of the press and certain political quarters. He was not only tolerated but was even feted among many Europeans while the settlers in the Taranaki District endured years of 'unease' (sic) because of the Government's prevarication in acting against Te Whit's obstructionist tactics.

Governor Sir Arthur Gordon, for example, regarded Te Whiti with the utmost favour, and viciously slandered Native Minister John Bryce, who had commanded the colonial forces occupying Parihaka. As early as the 1880s the myth of Te Whiti and Parihaka had begun to take shape with the book *The Groans of the Maoris* by historian and jurist G W Rusden, who sought to portray the Maori in general and Te Whiti in particular in a sympathetic light[1] While the press often described Te Whiti as insane, this was not a universal opinion, and others of the colonialist media portrayed Te Whiti in the same saintly fashion as he is portrayed today. Governors and Premiers called on Parihaka to try and gain Te Whiti's favour, while the settlers of Taranaki suffered from continual vandalism and intimidation by his followers.

Maori and Pakeha with political and economic interests have resurrected Parihaka as a contemporary symbol. The myth is promoted in schools, by government agencies, via books, film,

---

1   Rusden, p. 41.

and the arts. The iconic New Zealand 'artist' Colin McCahon[2] made Parihaka the subject of one of his ridiculous daubings. The Govett-Brewster Art Gallery, New Plymouth, which holds the revered paint-smears 'in trust for the people of Parihaka', helps to perpetuate the Parihaka Myth in its description of the McCahon work with arrant nonsense typical of the myth:

> Colin McCahon's *Parihaka triptych* is a response to one of the most shameful episodes in Aotearoa New Zealand's colonial history: the 1881 invasion and destruction of the peaceful Māori settlement of Parihaka by government militia. Two rangatira, Te Whiti o Rongomai and Tohu Kākahi, established Parihaka as a site of non-violent resistance to government land confiscations in Taranaki. A popular movement emerged at Parihaka based around Te Whiti and Tohu's teachings, which combined a vast reservoir of traditional Māori knowledge with insights gleaned from Christianity. McCahon's compelling work is a monument to these two leaders, painted to honour their legacy, vision and spiritual authority…. McCahon gifted the Parihaka triptych to the people of Parihaka and it is held in trust by the Govett-Brewster. Inscribed with both English and Māori text, it addresses diverse audiences, concluding with the hope that Te Whiti and Tohu's legacy may live on.[3]

Virginia Winder, when writing for the New Plymouth District Council, indicates the official status bestowed on the Parihaka Myth and Te Whiti:

> Imagine a leader so inspiring he is able to encourage men with warrior hearts to stand up for their rights, while laying

---

2   The Govett-Brewster Art Gallery describes McCahon thus: 'Colin McCahon (1919-1987) is widely recognised as New Zealand's foremost painter. Over 45 years his work encompassed many themes, subjects and styles, from landscape to figuration to abstraction and an innovative use of painted text. His adaption [sic] of aspects of modernist painting to a specific local situation and his intense engagement with spiritual matters, mark him out as a distinctive figure in twentieth century art'.
3   Govett-Brewster Art Gallery, Parihaka Triptych 1972.

down their weapons. Picture this same man convincing 2000 people to welcome battle-thirsty soldiers into their village, and even offer them food and drink. Even more surprising is how this peaceful leader allows himself and his people to be arrested without showing the slightest shrug of resistance.[4]

Winder evokes the spirit of Gandhi in describing Te Whiti as a 'great leader'. She states that the spirit of Parihaka is undergoing a renaissance:

You may believe you are reading the story of famous pacifist Mahatma Gandhi, of India, or another of the world's great leaders. But in fact, this is the tale of a man from Aotearoa/New Zealand. Te Whiti o Rongomai III was the leader of Parihaka, a Maori village nestled in a lahar-lumpy landscape between Mount Taranaki and the Tasman Sea. Even though Te Whiti died in 1907, his spirit of peace is still alive at the slowly reviving kainga (village)- and way beyond...[5]

Winder quotes 'Parihaka historian' Te Miringa Hohaia, that: 'We had Mahatma Gandhi, Martin Luther-King, Nelson Mandela and Te Whiti o Rongomai... Te Whiti was the forerunner of them all'. Winder adds: 'Even now Te Whiti's name is associated with justice, peace and freedom for oppressed people'.[6]

The sanctity around Parihaka has been given official status as a major part of New Zealand history, with the Human Rights Commission stating in regard to the annual Parihaka International Peace Festival: 'The events that took place in and around Parihaka particularly from about 1860 to 1900 have affected the political, cultural and spiritual dynamics of the entire country'.[7]

---

4   Winder, May 27, 2003.
5   *Ibid.*
6   *Ibid.*
7   Human Rights Commission, 2010.

III - Cult Religion

The cult founded by Te Whiti was called *Raukura*. The word refers to albatross feathers, which were worn as a symbol of commitment to Te Whiti. In Parihaka tradition the 'prophet' Tohu had seen an albatross flying overhead. This was regarded as symbolising the holy spirit.[1] While Ms Winder refers to Te Whiti's beliefs as being based on a synthesis of 'traditional values and knowledge, mixed with some Christianity', given the added ingredient of delusional *messianism*, a more dispassionate description might suggest a cult with Te Whiti as a Jim Jones type figure. Despite the Christ-like status accorded to Te Whiti, Christianity was not a major ingredient of his belief system, Winder quoting Te Miringa Hohaia:

> He showed qualities that were close to Godliness, but I can't say he was a religious man. He was buried without a Christian ceremony. That was his own wish. I don't see a row of churches that were built down the coast by Te Whiti and Tohu. There wasn't even a church at Parihaka.[2]

However, despite not being a Christian, Te Whiti's 'favourite' book, according to Winder, was *Revelations*. However, Te Whiti also especially utilised the *Old Testament*, a favourite of cult figures because of the numerous references to divine vengeance and 'chosen people'. In the manner reminiscent of modern cult figures such as Jim Jones, David Koresh or Moses David, Te Whiti portrayed his followers as an elect people surrounded by a hostile world. Like a Maori Jeremiah he laid down that he was their Prophet, revealing to them the Word of God that, if

---

1   The Taranaki Report, 8.3.
2   Winder, op. cit.

obeyed, would result in their salvation, but if ignored would end in their destruction. Winder quotes Te Whiti to his followers in 1881, apparently without seeing anything disturbing about the character of her subject:

> My word to you to the tribe... There are two roads, one to life and one to death. God said, in the days of Noah, the earth will be destroyed; build an ark, or all will perish. Noah did as he was commanded and this was an example for us to follow. God said to Lot, depart from the city; leave your houses and goods, for he who turns back shall die, and the city shall be burnt. This is an example for us to follow. God said to Moses, do not strive against me, or you will die; by faith only can this tribe be saved. This also is an example to us. Our salvation today is stout-heartedness and patience ...[3]

There are, from a psychological viewpoint, many aspects of this passage indicating the nature of Te Whiti's frequent revelations:

> 'My word to you to the tribe' opens the speech in a revelatory manner.

> Like the Old Testament Prophets, Te Whiti offers up 'two roads', the one of salvation that is being offered by the Prophet, or the one of destruction if the people stray from the Prophet's word.

> Those who follow Te Whiti, and specifically who renounce their possessions and settle at Parihaka as the Promised Land if they stay faithful, will survive Armageddon.

---

3   *Ibid.*, Te Whiti, November 1, 1881.

Lost Tribes of Israel

In Te Whiti's interpretation of the Old Testament, the Maori are descendents of Ham while the Pakeha are from Japhet. Te Whiti regarded Titokowaru and his people as the tribe of Benjamin.[4] This is of added interest insofar as Titokowaru was a particularly vicious warrior chief, with his own cult that included ritual cannibalism. Historian Keith Sinclair states that Titokowaru was probably in alliance with Te Whiti even when still engaged in violence. Sinclair writes that Te Whiti quoted the Old Testament in describing the tribe of Benjamin: 'Benjamin shall ravine as a wolf: in the morning he shall devour the prey, and at night he shall divide the spoil'. (*Genesis*: 49: 27).[5] It is also notable that well-known New Zealand historian James Belich, whose book on Titokowaru has recently been republished, does not so much as mention the cult of ritual cannibalism that Titokowaru led.[6]

Considering the identification of Titokowaru and his warriors as the Old Testament tribe of Benjamin, Te Whiti seems to have been choosing Titokowaru as the instrument of his divine judgement in a physical war, for which Titokowaru and his war cult were notorious. Perhaps the interpretation of yet another enigmatic statement by Te Whiti, that 'there will be peace, but a different kind of peace, it will be a fighting peace'[7] can be judged in terms of a 'spiritual peace' promised for Te Whiti's followers, but achieved through the instrument of Titokowaru's 'Benjaminites' as they 'devour the prey', and 'divide the spoil'.

Traits of Cult Leader

The demands by Te Whiti on his followers have the primary elements of cultic control, such as that used by Jim Jones to isolate his followers from the corrupt world about them and surrender everything they have to form a remote community in the jungles

4   Sinclair, p. 74.
5   *Ibid.*, p. 75.
6   J Belich, I Shall Not Die: Titokowaru's War. New Zealand 1868-1869.
7   Riseborough, p. 231.

of Guyana. At the isolated Jonestown commune Jones announced that this would be the sanctuary for the elect in a future nuclear holocaust, and often warned his followers of an impending attack against them, which might require their mass suicide. Jones, with his synthesis of revelatory Biblical *messianism* and Marxism believed himself to be the reincarnation of Lenin. When Jones died his personal assets were reported to have been $5,000,000 while his followers were kept in poverty, a requirement being that they turn their possessions and assets over to The Reverend. Jones' wife Marcelina stated that Jones never believed in Christianity but was a Marxist who used religion as a means of control. Because of his sales pitch as a minister helping the poor, and especially appealing to multi-racialism, he was courted by local politicians, including the Governor of California, and the mayors of San Francisco and Los Angels, and was invited to meet Vice President Walter Mondale.[8] This is the typical reflex of liberal politicians who are overly eager to embrace any and every cause that denigrates or undermines the Caucasian[9], whether it is the lauding of Te Whiti even during the supposed era of 19th Century 'colonial oppression', or today's sanctification of Nelson Mandela and the disposing of his terrorist past[10] down the Memory Hole, while lauding the hell-hole of post-apartheid South Africa as an ebullient 'rainbow nation'. There are significant comparisons between the Te Whiti and Jim Jones cults:

> Te Whiti sought to attract Maori from far afield, subverting traditional tribal loyalties, bringing them under his authority, with Parihaka as the sanctuary where the righteous would survive a coming Armageddon in which the wicked would die. Parihaka was analogous to Jonestown.

> Te Whiti, like Jones, expected material tributes, receiving vast quantities of food, goods and money from his

---

8   Schoeder, p. 123.
9   Jones's 'People's Temple' was hyped as a paragon of multiculturalism; an example of how all races could live in harmony.
10 Terrorist Watch, 'Mandela and the Church Street Bombing'.

followers to the point where they denuded and neglected their own settlements, paying for the privilege of attending the increasingly frequent feats at Parihaka. That is, they had to pay for the privilege of eating their own food. Te Whiti's fortune was estimated as £60,000.

Te Whiti used religious rhetoric to promote his political aims, presenting his people and himself as persecuted for the sake of God by a wicked world.

One might wonder why Te Whiti is today depicted with reverence by academics who would otherwise describe such a figure as a 'psychotic cult leader'? As the reader considers Te Whiti's character, his paranoid reactions towards the outside world, his messiah-complex, and his feelings of persecution, comparison might be made with the traits typical of a sociopathic cult leader:

Let us look for a moment at how some of this manifests in the cult leader. Cult leaders have an outstanding ability to charm and win over followers. They beguile and seduce. They enter a room and garner all the attention. They command the utmost respect and obedience. These are 'individuals whose narcissism is so extreme and grandiose that they exist in a kind of splendid isolation in which the creation of the grandiose self takes precedence over legal, moral or interpersonal commitments'. Paranoia may be evident in simple or elaborate delusions of persecution. Highly suspicious, they may feel conspired against, spied upon or cheated, or maligned by a person, group, or governmental agency. Any real or suspected unfavorable reaction may be interpreted as a deliberate attack upon them or the group.

Harder to evaluate, of course, is whether these leaders' belief in their magical powers, omnipotence, and connection to God (or whatever higher power or belief system they are espousing) is delusional or simply part of the con. Megalomania - the belief that one is able or entitled to rule the world - is equally hard to evaluate without psychological testing of the individual, although numerous cult leaders state quite readily that their goal is to rule the world. In any case, beneath the surface gloss of intelligence, charm, and professed humility seethes an inner world of rage, depression, and fear.[11]

Prophecies of Death and Salvation

In 1882 Te Whiti prophesied that the 'Great Comet'[12] which appeared over Mt. Egmont (or Mt. Taranaki as it is now called) would fulfil his prophecies about the end of the world. A contemporary newspaper account explained:

> The comet will decide who are good and who are bad in the world, and he advises all good people, both Maoris and Pakehas, to go to Parihaka and wait for the coming end of all things. The bad people he advises to keep away from Parihaka, as they would only contaminate the good, and would bring down greater vengeance on their own heads.[13]

Salvation from death could hence only be attained through recognition of the divine status of Te Whiti and the holy ground of Parihaka. Those who did not submit to Te Whiti and come to Parihaka would perish, but the presence of the unholy at Parihaka would bring down a worse judgement. Here again is the cultist characteristic of the messiah declaring his domain to be the sanctuary from evil and from the end of the world. The depiction of the 'Great Comet' as a sign of impending apocalypse recalls the cult Heaven's Gate, centred on the comet Hale-Bopp.[14] In a manner similar to Heaven's Gate leader Applewhite, Te Whiti

---

11   Madeleine Landau, Tobias and Janja Lalich, Captive Hearts, Captive Minds.
12   *Taranaki Herald*, 1883, p. 2.
13   Otago Daily Times, 1882, p. 2.
14   Schroedder, op. cit., p. 136.

also foretold his approaching martyrdom, Christ-like, and it might be contended that he set a course in motion that was intended to result in the fulfilment of this 'prophecy'. A report in the *Nelson Evening Mail* stated:

> Patea, Friday. Te Whiti predicts that a large host will surround Parihaka and take him prisoner and that the Maoris will not resist. He will then be put to death, but on the third day he will rise again from the dead and the Pakehas will fall down and worship him but all Pakeha sinners will be destroyed. Katene says there is no pah inland of Parihaka and the Natives themselves say that Te Whiti is their pah and their stronghold.[15]

Te Whiti conducted himself in an intransigent manner, and refused all Government attempts to negotiate or to explain the land that was to be set-aside for Maori. His speech for the Parihaka gathering in September 1881, several months prior to the colonial occupation, was provocative and ambiguous in regard to violence, spoken in 'metaphors' that were easily interpreted as a 'declaration of war'. *Te Whiti spent years dedicated to provoking as confrontation with the authorities that would fulfil his own prophecies of martyrdom.* That, in a sentence, is the whole premise of the Parihaka myth.

In 1879, the year of his prediction of Christ-like martyrdom, it was reported in regard to Te Whiti refusing to hand over the chief Hikori for trial for murder, that Te Whiti had stated his followers would continue ploughing up any European land they wanted to occupy, and 'that the European had not the power to prevent the Natives from doing so....' Te Whiti had instilled in his followers a belief that the Pakeha did not have the power to 'fire a shot in Parihaka'.[16] Such claims are analogous to those of the Muslim *mahdi* and the American Indian Ghost Dance cult, and indeed to

---

15   *Nelson Evening Mail*, 1879, p. 2.
16   *Wanganui Herald*, 1879, p. 2.

the previous Maori Hau Hau cult that was led by Te Whiti's later ally, Titokowaru. At the September 1879 Parihaka gathering Te Whiti alluded to himself as the lord who would be recognised by both Maori and Pakeha, and said that his followers who had been jailed would not return until he called them supernaturally, even should the doors be opened.[17]

In November 1881, days before the occupation of Parihaka by the Constabulary, when the atmosphere was particularly tense, Te Whiti again prophesied his ending in terms typical of the cult leader, reminiscent of how Jim Jones addressed his followers prior to their mass-suicide: he was the wronged and persecuted messiah who wanted nothing but good, but could not be left alone by the evil world about him. Te Whiti declared:

> What matters it? My object is accomplished; peace reigns. I am willing to become a sacrifice for my object.... Oh, hard-hearted people! I am here to be taken. Take me for the sins of the island! Why hesitate? Am I not here? Though I am killed, I yet shall live; and, though dead, will yet live in my object—which is peace. The future is mine, and little children will answer in the future when questioned as to the author of peace; they will say, Te Whiti, and I will bless them.[18]

The academic, Rusden, writing during the 19th Century, even then saw nothing amiss in regard to Te Whiti's statements about martyrdom, but lambasted the colonial administration.

Compare the above passages of Te Whiti's messianic and apocalyptic speeches with that of Jim Jones' final address to his followers preceding the mass suicides at Jonestown. Among much else that is garbled, disjointed and symptomatic of psychosis, we read:

---

17   Otago Daily Times, 1879, p. 3.
18   Rusden, p. 11.

I have never, never, never, never seen anything like this before in my life. I've never seen people take the law and do - in their own hands and provoke us and try to purposely agitate mother of children...

I tried to give it to you. I've laid down my life, practically. I've practically died every day to give you peace. And you still not have any peace. You look better than I've seen you in a long while, but it's still not the kind of peace that I want to give you... I've saved them. I saved them, but I made my example. I made my expression. I made my manifestation, and the world was ready, not ready for me. Paul said, 'I was a man born out of due season'. I've been born out of due season, just like all we are, and the best testimony we can make is to leave this goddamn world...

Some months I've tried to keep this thing from happening. But I now see it's the will—it's the will of Sovereign Being that this happen to us. That we lay down our lives to protest against what's being done. That we lay down our lives to protest at what's being done. The criminality of people. The cruelty of people...

Who walked out of here today? See all those who walked out? Mostly white people. Mostly white people walked. I'm so grateful for the ones that didn't - those who knew who they are. I just know that there's no point – there's no point to this. We are born before our time. They won't accept us. And I don't think we should sit here and take any more time for our children to be endangered. Because if they come after our children, and we give them our children, then our children will suffer forever... They've robbed us of our land, and they've taken us and driven us and we tried to find ourselves.[19]

---

19   J Jones, 'Suicide Tape Transcript'.

Both Jones and Te Whiti saw themselves as persecuted messiahs, who had worked for peace but who had been spurned and betrayed by the sinful world; who were willing to lay down their lives, who prophesied that their fates were not of their making. All the elements between the two are the same, yet Jones' sociopathy could not be justified even by his former liberal sycophants. However Te Whiti's façade of peace and goodwill are still being maintained by claims that he was misunderstood. There were no deaths at the Parihaka occupation because of the forbearance of the colonial troops. However, as Te Whiti made sufficiently clear in his statements long preceding the showdown with the Government, he sought to provoke a confrontation as the fulfilment of his self-portrayal as a prophet and a messiah who would die and rise from the dead to lead his people in a new dispensation against the whites. Like Jones, he was willing to sacrifice the lives of his followers to fulfil his destiny.

Jones provoked a crisis by dispatching his 'elite' to kill Congressman Leo Ryan et al as they were about to embark on a plane back to the USA. Jones told his followers that nothing of this had been of his making; he and they were the victims, and the world was not good enough for them.[20] Typical of the sociopath, Te Whiti also shifted responsibility from himself onto the Government for a confrontation he had been trying to provoke and had been predicting for years. Jim Jones is remembered as a lunatic, while Te Whiti is upheld as a paragon of peace and justice by national and local government bodies.

Raising the Dead

While Te Whiti achieved obedience by instilling the belief that he had supernatural powers to heal and to resurrect the dead, he was also believed to have the power to kill by supernatural means. After a relative of Te Whiti's, Pihana, who had been appointed as Native Assessor at Parihaka by the Native Minister, later fell

20   *Ibid.*

from his horse and died, Te Whiti, 'At a large meeting held on Saturday... made a capital speech out of the accident, and quoted the case as an example of his miraculous power and the evil which would befall natives who worked against him'.[21] Just how this is supposed to be the outlook of a 'pacifist' is difficult to interpret.

1879 seems to have been a year in which Te Whiti instructed his followers to act in a particularly aggressive manner, but since they did not carry guns on their forays, the legend of 'passive resistance' is maintained. Was this increased offensive against settler property a means of mollifying dissatisfaction with Te Whiti? That year two tribes left Parihaka, having become disillusioned with prophecies that were not being fulfilled, and Te Whiti was denounced as a 'deceiver'.[22] In 1880 there was dissatisfaction that Te Whiti and Tohu had permitted the jailing of 59 followers. Tohu attempted to counter this by claiming supernatural powers in healing, stating that he had restored sight to a blind man.[23]

In 1879 Te Whiti's followers caused a fracas at a general store, indicative of the type of attitude that the settlers were obliged to cope with while the Government prevaricated, the *Nelson Evening Mail* reporting:

> Yesterday a party of twelve Maoris, when returning from Parihaka, entered Loveridge's store at Oakura, commenced pulling the things about, and were very bounceable. The Constabulary had to be called in to eject them.[24]

When commenting on Te Whiti, no thought is given to the plight of the settlers, working under a state of continual 'unease', eking out a fragile existence for their families under the shadow of Parihaka while the Government tried for years to appease Te Whiti.

---

21   *Poverty Bay Herald*, 1879, p. 2.
22   *Grey River Argus*, 1879, p. 2.
23   Evening Post, 1880, p. 3.
24   *Nelson Evening Mail*, 1879, p. 2.

Paying Homage

In the manner that is often a feature of the cult leader, there was much effort from Te Whiti's followers to give gifts of money, goods and livestock to their prophet and messiah. Lt. Col. Roberts, reporting on the Parihaka meetings for June 1885 to the Under-Secretary of the Native Office, observed that,

> On the 22nd Titokowaru and his party presented various sums of money, amounting altogether to 47 pound, to Te Whiti. The party, marching in Indian file, passed Te Whiti's house, each depositing his gift on a table.[25]

Roberts reported that an old chief came forward and declared he was fed up with the continual requests for money:

> On the 25th, at the request of Te Whiti, Titokowaru's party performed a haka in the marae, all the Maoris meeting to witness it, and at the conclusion 68 pound was collected. Immediately after an old chief of Parihaka stood up and made the following speech: 'This is June. June was to be the month, the 18th (our 17th) is gone. My ears are tired, nothing has been said but "beg, beg, for money"', and I am sick of it.' Nothing was replied to this.[26]

Of the meeting for the 29th June, Roberts wrote:

> That Te Whiti's influence over them is as great as ever is shown by the means which they adopt to procure money to present to him; horses, cattle, and other property being sold to obtain it. There are large quantities of food at Parihaka, such as potatoes and the usual kind of Maori food; but at all their feasts at this meeting they endeavoured to copy the European meals, preserved milk even being procured from the stores, and everything was carried out in true pakeha style...[27]

---

25 Roberts, 1885.
26 *Ibid.*
27 *Ibid.*

In 1887 Te Whiti was presented with 2000 cattle at a special gathering that drew Maori from far and wide, making him a cattleman of considerable substance.[28]

Subverting Traditional Loyalties

Te Whiti maintained command over his followers by replacing traditional chiefly structures. Parris, the long-serving District Commissioner who maintained a sympathetic attitude and even friendship towards Te Whiti to an extent that seems unmerited by his own account of Te Whiti's character, reported to the Undersecretary of the Native Department in 1882:

> The old custom of chiefs having authority over the respective *Hapus* and tribal interests was completely abolished, as was forcibly exemplified to the Hon. the late Premier, Mr. Hall, on the occasion of his passing through the district with me last year, when we met on the road an old chief, with whom we had a conversation about the state of things in general, in the course of which the old man said: 'formerly chiefs had a potent voice in everything, but now they are nonentities; all authority is now vested in Te Whiti, you must talk to him'.[29]

Parris observed that when the meetings at Parihaka, which attracted Maori from afar, became monthly rather than twice-yearly, the attendees were required to bring vast quantities of their own food regardless of the consequences to themselves, 'although indigence was inevitable by so doing, believing it was their duty to part with all they had for such time as might be necessary for the final consummation of Te Whiti's prophecies, when, as he gave them to understand, everything would be restored to them by some mysterious process'. Parris observed that Te Whiti told his followers he was Jehovah and all their

28   *Taranaki Herald*, 1887, p. 2.
29   Parris, 1881, G1, No. 10.

time was devoted to maintaining Parihaka, adding that Te Whiti could have made very good terms with the Government on the land question, but was not interested in doing so.[30]

Parris states in his report that Te Whiti demanded of his followers, coming in from the furthest reaches of the district, that they deposit their crops at Parihaka for the monthly meetings. After those who had settled at Parihaka from elsewhere – the majority - were dispersed back to their homes following Bryce's raid in November 1881, it became a problem as to how they were going to sustain themselves back in their own settlements, which had been neglected for years.[31] It was this neglect of Maori communities, because of the demands of Te Whiti, that was of particular concern for the Government, and one of the primary reasons for the removal of Maori from Parihaka back to their own communities by Bryce when he occupied Parihaka. Maori settlements were being denuded of people and crops as Te Whiti sought to break up traditional tribal ties and re-forge a new nation under his own authority. For example, Maori at Makai, near Hawera, sold off their stocks and moved to Parihaka, leaving just one elderly chief.[32] Rent from the reserves of other *hapu* was also given to Te Whiti's coffers, *The Poverty Bay Herald* commenting on this in 1879:

> It is rumoured that Hane Pihatia has now a leaning towards Te Whiti, and is sending supplies of threshed corn grown by him near Nomanby to Parihaka. Hone Pihana also ordered all the natives over whom he has influence, and who are in receipt of rent from the reserves to pay the same to Te Whiti.[33]

Land was even sold to the Government to pay for large quantities of crockery for a banquet in 1885 in honour of Te Whiti. Since

---

30   *Ibid.*
31   *Ibid.*
32   *Poverty Bay Herald*, 1879, p. 2.
33   *Ibid.*

the country stores could not meet the quantities required, a party travelled to Wellington where an advance was requested to buy 300 cups and saucers, 100 plates and other items.[34]

In cultic manner, Te Whiti was widely believed to be immortal by his followers. After he died many, particularly among the elderly, believed he would be resurrected.[35]

Te Whiti would not allow religious rivalry in his domain. Although receiving Bishops as a display of his *mana*[36] proselytising by missionaries was not permitted.[37] Te Whiti maintained an apocalyptic interpretation of events, typical of cult leaders who instil collective paranoia among their followers. In 1897 he stated to Peter Buck, the future noted scholar who was then translating newspapers for Te Whiti, that Premier Richard Seddon, who had gone to Britain to attend the celebration of Queen Victoria's Diamond Jubilee, was actually there to receive permission from the Sovereign to exterminate the Maori.[38]

Te Whiti had all the primary characteristics of what is now recognized as those of a cult leader, but despite what is now known by psychology and cult studies, no such methodology has been applied in assessing Te Whiti.

---

34   *Bay Of Plenty Times*, 1885, p. 2.
35   *Grey River Argus*, 1911, p. 1.
36   Mana = power, authority, *Maori Dictionary*, http://www.maoridictionary.co.nz/
37   Observer, 1883, p. 2.
38   Sinclair, p. 71.

IV - Land Wars

Parihaka as the centre of Maori resistance had its origins in the 1860s when meetings would be held on the 18th and 19th of every month to commemorate the start of the first Taranaki Land War of 1860. The practice continued even after the deaths of Te Whiti and his rival Tohu in 1907, and today there is an annual Parihaka International Peace Festival.

Parihaka as a settlement was, however, founded by a part-Maori gold-miner, Daniel Ellison, a.k.a. Raniera Erihana, who made almost a million pounds at the Dunstan diggings in Central Otago. Ellison married the granddaughter of Ngai Tahu chief Taiaroa in 1861, according to Ngai Tahu historian, Jean Jackson.[1] He encouraged squatters to settle at Parihaka, and sunk his money into it. Jackson remarks: 'Until the 1860s it seems there was no Parihaka, the village often misrepresented, built near New Plymouth. The settlement was largesse… from Raniera Erihana or Daniel Ellison'.[2]

It is here necessary to state something of the context of the Taranaki Land War since this is the cause of Maori grievances, which continue to the present day.

Treaty of Waitangi

Maori land ownership is not the same as the present Western concept. This conceptual discrepancy has not only caused, since the first land purchases, much misunderstanding, but was – and continues to be - used as a means for outright swindling. The

---

1   Jean Jackson, 'A Strange Parihaka Bubble: Part of Taranaki's Saga'.
2   *Ibid.*

enigma of Maori land ownership necessitated the 'Treaty of Waitangi' in 1840, Maori Land Courts, and the present Waitangi Tribunal, causing billions of dollars often in payment and re-payment for what are farcically-termed 'final settlements'.

Between 1820 and 1840 the 'Musket Wars' between Maori tribes were instigated by Ngaphui chief Hongi Hika as *utu*[3] for a major Ngaphui defeat in 1807. Hongi Hika's onslaught resulted in approximately 60,000 deaths of Maori. Much of the North Island Maori had been decimated until in 1840 Maori chiefs appealed for the intervention of the British Crown. Although the British Parliament was reluctant to extend British sovereignty, there was concern at French interest in the country by both Parliament and Maori. In 1837 the possibility of stability became even more remote when war broke out between rivals of the Confederation of United Chiefs. Captain Hobson, sent to protect British settlers caught between Maori tribal fighting, recommended establishing a colony.

Acceding to Maori requests, the 'Treaty of Waitangi' was signed by Hobson for the Crown and by 512 Maori chiefs from both North and South Islands, who turned over their sovereignty in exchange for British protection. While it has been contended that the Maori and British conceptions of 'sovereignty' are different, and that there was never an intent by the Maori to give-away their sovereignty to the Crown, the contention is not new and was addressed by the celebrated Maori lawyer and politician Sir Apirana Ngata in 1922 when he wrote a Maori language explanation of the Treaty. Here he answered those who were trying to maintain that its terms meant something quite different than what was intended or understood by Maori.

Sir Apirana insisted that Maori sovereignty in the full political sense was ceded to the Crown. It was 'chiefly authority' that was ceded to the Crown, meaning all authority from the chiefs; 'the

---

3   Revenge, often applied as collective guilt against an entire hapu, perpetrated for generations, and generally resulting in counter-utu. *Maori Dictionary.*

power even of life and death', their control over the land and of the making of laws.[4]

The Second Article of the Treaty, that of assuring possession of the lands other than when Maori accede to selling via the Crown, also remains a major contention, as it is claimed that the intent of the Treaty was to guarantee Maori land ownership on which Colonial and subsequent administrations have reneged. Therefore Maori have argued that when the State confiscates land it contravenes the Treaty. Sir Apirana commented, 'This has given rise to wishful thinking on the part of many Maori groups... All this wishful thinking goes back to this article of the Treaty'.[5] Ngata stated that at the time of the Treaty the Maori chiefs had partitioned all the lands and were disputing the titles and boundaries, resulting in much bloodshed. The Maori Land Court was established to resolve such disputes peaceably, while providing for sale of lands to the Crown in a legal manner.[6] The Maori Land Act of 1862 provided for the Government to enquire into the genuine ownership of lands, although this has never been a simple process. The chaotic state of tribal claims to ownership resulted in the fraudulent multiple sale of land to Government, and prior to 1840 to settlers and to the New Zealand Company by a multiplicity of parties contending true 'ownership'. Ngata comments:

> Many claims were made by various Europeans for the one piece of land sold to each of them by various Maori chiefs. Where was the law in those times to decide what was right?[7]

---

4   Ngata, p. 6.
5   *Ibid.*, p. 8).
6   *Ibid.*
7   *Ibid.*, p. 4).

'Full and Final Settlements'?

Many of the 'full and final settlements' to the present day had already been concluded under the Treaty and had gone through 'full and final settlements' many times over during the course of over a century.[8] In another generation there will be demands for more 'full and final settlements'...Selling land that does not belong to one, or reselling it on multiple occasions, is generally regarded as a 'con', but it is a 'con' that continues behind the façade of righteous indignation about alleged colonial oppression, dispossession and illegal confiscations.

In connection with the alleged injustices inflicted on the Maori, Ngata points out that Maori land was not subjected to rates until 1894, and then at only half that of the rest of New Zealand. Not until 1910 was Maori land rated on par with Pakeha land, and was not taxed until 1893, at half the tax payable by Pakeha.[9]

In regard to confiscated lands which have a specific bearing on the riotous behaviour from Te Whiti's followers, Ngata stated that: 'Some have said that these confiscations were wrong and that they contravened the articles of the "Treaty of Waitangi"'. He states that confiscation was the result of 'some sections of the Maori people' having 'violated' the authority ceded by the chiefs to the Crown. 'War arose from this and blood was spilled. The law came into operation and land was taken in payment'.[10]

---

8   For example, in 2008 the Government achieved a 'full and final settlement' with seven North Island iwi for the purchase of nine Kaingaroa forests for half a billion dollars, 'an apology from the Crown', and an annual rental of $15,000,000. However the land had already been paid for, selling for £15,000 in 1879, when the esteemed Capt. Gilbert Mair (who was several years later at Parihaka with the Bryce raid) acting for the Government, reached a 'full and final settlement' (in today's parlance) with the owners, who were fully apprised on the meaning of the sale, and were very pleased with the payment. Mair recounted long after that he had 'explained at great length the irrevocable nature' of the sale. By illustration, he stated that while Kaingoroa meant 'the long enduring home,' if the land was sold it would henceforth be Kainga-poto; 'the quickly vanishing wealth'. It is evident that Mair tried to dissuade the Maori from selling. (Mair, 1879).

9   Ngata, p. 13.

10   *Ibid.*, p. 15.

Sale of Taranaki

Taranaki, the district that was contended by Te Whiti, had already been sold by supposed 'owners' at least five times to the New Zealand Company, to other settlers' organisations, or to the Hobson administration, and payment had been given in good faith and in full. Historian Martin Doutré comments:

> Every paramount chief of Taranaki, whether conquered, dispossessed and vanquished (like Wiremu Kingi) or the conqueror and new owner... were fully paid after formal negotiations for the land there and the sale agreement documents, signed by both willing settler-willing buyer, still languish in our archives. Despite this the British are still accused of theft.[11]

In 1839 the New Zealand Company purchased the Taranaki district from the two principal chiefs of the Ngatiawa. Col. Edward Gibbon Wakefield, director of the New Zealand Company, recorded that the Maori were eager that he should acquire the whole district so that the Ngatiawa could dwell there under the Company's protection without fear of the Waikato tribes. Wells writes in his definitive *History of Taranaki*:

> On 8th November, 1839, a deed was executed in Queen Charlotte's Sound, by which the Ngatiawa conveyed to the Company all the land from the Mokau river past Taranaki, Wanganui, and Wellington, to Cape Tikukahore, in latitude 41 deg. on the East Coast. This deed was personally signed by thirty Maoris, and two by proxy.[12]

The New Zealand Company found the same situation as that of the British administrations shortly after; that protection was sought by those who had been decimated by tribal warfare. However, the Waikato Maori threatened war, as they regarded

---

11   Doutré, p. 152.
12   Wells, p. 20.

Taranaki as theirs and not for the Ngatiawa to sell.[13] A 'liberal price' was therefore also given to Waikato chiefs for the acquisition of Taranaki although, due to tribal warfare, the land was virtually devoid of inhabitants.[14] Dr Ernest Diefenbach, the New Zealand Company's naturalist, wrote in his *Travels in New Zealand* (1843), as cited by Wells:

> Thus the New Zealand Company became proprietors of the finest district in New Zealand, which offers to the colonist, besides its natural resources, the advantage of there being no natives on the land, with the exception of the small remnant of the Ngatiawa tribe at Ngamotu.[15]

The deed of sale, signed 15 February 1840 reads:

> Know all men by these presents, that we the undersigned, chiefs of Ngamotu, near Mount Egmont, in New Zealand, have this day sold and parted with all our rights, titles, claims, and interests, in all the lands, islands, tenements, woods, bays, harbours, rivers, streams, and creeks, within certain boundaries, as shall be truly described in the deed, unto John Dorset, Esquire, his executors and administrators, in trust for the Governor, directors, and shareholders of the New Zealand Land Company, in London, their heirs, administrators, and assigns forever... And in order to prevent any dispute or misunderstanding, and to guarantee more fully unto the said Governors, directors, and shareholders, of the New Zealand Land Company of London, their heirs, administrators, and assigns forever, true, undisputed possession of the said lands, islands, tenements, woods, bays, harbours, rivers, streams and creeks, we, the said chiefs, for ourselves, families, tribes and successors forever, do hereby agree and bind ourselves to the description following, which

---

13   *Ibid.*, p. 38
14   *Ibid.*, p. 41.
15   *Ibid.*, p. 41.

constitutes the boundaries of the aforesaid lands, islands, tenements, woods, bays, harbours, rivers, streams and creeks, now sold by us, the undersigned chiefs, to the said John Dorset, this 15th day of February, in the year of our Lord, 1840, that is to say, from the mouth of the Wakatino river...

And we, the aforesaid chiefs, do hereby acknowledge for ourselves, families, tribes, and successors forever, to have this day received a full and sufficient payment for the aforesaid lands, islands, tenements, woods, bays, harbours, streams and creeks.

In witness whereof, the said Chiefs of the first part, and the said John Dorset of the second part, have hereunto put their hands and seals this 15th day of February, in the year of our Lord 1840.

Here follow 72 signatures of Maoris; also that of John Dorset, Acting Agent for the New Zealand Land Company.[16]

The intentions expressed in deeds of sale are thorough and clear. It is disingenuous to claim that Maori did not understand what they were signing away, either with such private deeds or under the Treaty.

Soon after, developments meant that the British Colonial Office did not recognise the New Zealand Company purchases, and it had become urgently necessary to gain New Zealand as a Crown colony in order to thwart the interests of France. Hence the 'Treaty of Waitangi'.[17] The Plymouth Company was now formed in England for the purpose of promoting colonisation, and land was purchased from the New Zealand Company.[18]

---

16   *Ibid.*, pp. 41-42.
17   *Ibid.*, pp. 43-44.
18   *Ibid.*, p. 59. The Plymouth Company soon had financial difficulties, and merged with the New Zealand Company.

The first ship of the Plymouth Company embarked for Taranaki in November 1840, landing at what became New Plymouth. The Plymouth Company officials had in particular sought settlers from agricultural and mining labourers from Cornwall.[19] These were families and individuals who came to New Zealand in the hope of a better life, and were willing to confront the unknown and work to cut out a homestead from the wilderness. They are the people now denigrated by agitators and academics alike as exploiters, rapists, pillagers, thieves and murderers.

In November 1841 Governor Sir George Gipps despatched to the British Secretary of State: 'At Taranaki the powerful tribe of Waikato threatens to dislodge the settlers, because they did not buy the land from them, they claiming it by right of conquest', although 'liberal payment', as mentioned, had already been made to Waikato tribes as well as to the Ngatiawa by the New Zealand Company. The following month Gipps wrote: 'Now Te Wherowhero claims Taranaki by right of conquest, and insists that the remnant of the Ngatiawa are slaves; that they live at Taranaki by sufferance, and that they have no right whatever to sell the land without his consent'.[20]

Therefore, after receiving a party from the Waikato under Te Kaka, the Taranaki land was paid for again, this time by the Colonial administration, the deed of sale again clearly stating:

Know all men by this paper, that we, chiefs of Waikato, do let go and sell these lands of ours to George Clarke, the protector of natives, for Her Majesty, the Queen of England, her heirs and successors, whether male or female; the land, and all things that are on or under this land, we sell to George Clarke, the protector of natives, for an estate for the Queen, her heirs and successors, whether male or female, forever.[21]

---

19   *Ibid.*, p. 59.
20   *Ibid.*, p. 77.
21   *Ibid.*

Many of those that had been enslaved by the Waikato Maori were being released and were returning to Taranaki, which had been left denuded of a native population. They were now complaining that they had not been party to the sale of land, while on the other hand the Waikato Maori were saying that the land was theirs by right of conquest, and no dealings should be made with the returning ex-slaves. John T Wicksteed, the Resident Agent for the New Zealand Company, wrote to Wakefield:

> The native reserves are sufficient for a population twenty-fold larger than that likely under any circumstances to belong to Taranaki; and I cannot discover among the malcontents a single person who, according to the custom of the natives, has or had a right to sell the land. On the contrary, many of those who did sell the land have distinctly warned me not to enter into any bargain or treaty with these returned slaves.[22]

These returning ex-slaves vented their anger against several peaceable settlers, but Wicksteed was able to amicably settle matters with the malcontents. On the other had, the Waikato Maori threatened to come into Taranaki and slaughter the remnant of the ex-slaves, but were placated with money from Wicksteed.[23] However, sporadic confrontations continued, as small groups of Maori attempted to arbitrarily fence off and cultivate Pakeha reserves.[24]

In June 1843 twenty Pakeha were killed while attempting to arrest two chiefs suspected of arson. The decision of the Colonial administration was that all disputes over land should be subjected to Crown determination, and Pakeha claims of ownership would be delayed until such time as being adjudicated.

The primary point of contention however remained the hostility

---

22   Wicksteed to Wakefield, July 25, 1842; cited by Wells, *Ibid.*, p. 86.
23   *Ibid.*, p. 91.
24   *Ibid.*, p. 92.

between the Waikato tribes and their ex-slaves, and the New Zealand Company declared itself in favour of protecting the locals from the threats of the Waikato. The New Zealand Company Resident Agent made it clear that the local natives were under Pakeha protection.[25] In reality, the Colonial administration had left those settlers with New Zealand Company purchases powerless to act even in self-defence, despite the vandalism and theft of settler property.

On 16 April, 1844 the Commissioner for land claims settlements, William Spain, convened a hearing and determined that the New Zealand Company was entitled to a Crown Grant of 60,000 acres, excluding all pa, burial grounds, various previously reserved lands, and lands already under Maori cultivation within the Crown Grant, in return for £200 for native benefit. However, this was over-ridden by Governor Fitzroy who instead determined that the Maori should receive £350 in goods, money and animals, for a block of land around New Plymouth, comprising 3,500 acres.[26] Wells comments in *The History of Taranaki*:

> After all the excellent speeches at Plymouth, after all the hopes that had been excited, after thousands of pounds had been spent, and hundreds of simple-hearted people had left their homes, traversed the seas, and established themselves in the wilderness, the settlement was diminished to the dimensions of a nobleman's park.[27]

Wells holds this betrayal of the settlers as being responsible for the Taranaki Land War. The Government had obliged the New Zealand Company to return the lands to the remnant of returned ex-slaves that had only been living in safety from the Waikato Maori by virtue of the protection of the Pakeha. The New Zealand Company had already purchased the land several times over, and then they were obliged to repurchase a mere fraction of it. Wells writes:

---

25   *Ibid.*, p. 97.
26   *Ibid.*, p. 107.
27   *Ibid.*, p. 108.

As soon as the Governor's decision was made known
the exulting Maoris commenced a series of persecutions
upon all the settlers who were living outside the lines of
the reduced settlement. One by one they sorrowfully came
in, abandoning their newly reclaimed fields, which soon
reverted to a state of nature...

To injury the Governor added insult; when the simple-
minded Devonshire and Cornish peasants attempted to
remonstrate with him and plead the cause of their families,
he told them they were all trespassers and deserved
transportation.[28]

It is the labouring classes of Britain who came to New Zealand
in good faith – with promises of a better future - and were caught
between Maori brutality and colonial prevarication that are
completely left out of the postmodernist historical narrative.

Taranaki War

Something of the nature of the land disputes and of the background
of intransigence and resistance which developed in Parihaka can
be ascertained from the antagonism created when District Agent
Parris paid Te Teira et al a £100 instalment to purchase their
lands at Waitara. In 1860 Wi Kingi of Waitara arrived at New
Plymouth with an escort of thirty to oppose the payment, and
although admitting to Parris that the land was that of Te Teira's,
Wi Kingi stated he would oppose the purchase. When Wi Kingi
prevented the surveying of the land he was given a twenty-
four hour ultimatum by the Government. Kingi persisted in his
obstruction, built a pa, and colonial troops occupied the area.
The conflict became the infamous Taranaki War and lasted for a
year, with Kingi calling on the Waikato Maori for support. Kingi
was defeated and signed a peace treaty in April 1861. After ten
years of living in seclusion Kingi went to Parihaka.[29] Wi Kingi's

28   *Ibid.*, p. 108.
29   *Ibid.*, p. 108. Wells described Kingi as 'a blusterer and a coward'.

tactics were repeated by Te Whiti. These included the use of women and children for purposes of obstruction, and posturing about not wanting conflict.[30] Wi Kingi was Te Whiti's mentor and had been known as Wiremu Kingi Whiti.[31]

Conflict erupted again in 1863, and the Te Teira purchase had still not been completed.[32]

The final excess of the Taranaki War came on 13 February 1869, when a war party of the Ngatimaniapoto attacked the British blockhouse at White Cliffs. Two Pakeha, who were enticed out of the blockhouse by Maori on the pretext of wanting to sell pigs, were killed. Lt. Gascoigne and his wife and three children, who had been in the cornfield, were tomahawked to death, as were their dog and cat.[33] The elderly missionary Mr Whiteley, who had spent years devoting his life to the Maori, was shot on approaching the blockhouse. The remains were discovered mutilated, including the children aged five years, three years and three months.[34] Taranaki was left destitute, and the Colonial troops were withdrawn. Many settlers had fled. The development of the district which caused Te Whiti to launch his campaign of obstruction followed nine years of warfare, depopulation and economic crisis.

These acts of war, arising from contentions between Maori, resulted in an Act for the confiscation of lands of rebel tribes as of 1 January 1863 as compensation.[35] Sir Apirana Ngata, in his previously cited document explaining the 'Treaty of Waitangi', maintained in 1922 that such confiscations were fully justified as reparations.[36]

---

30 *Ibid.*, p. 189.
31 Jean Jackson, op. cit.
32 *Ibid.*, p. 236.
33 One might here be reminded of the present-day actions of the followers of another messianic leader once feted by governing circles in many Western countries, Robert Mugabe, whose 'Zimbabwe veterans' have performed similar acts on the families of white farmers, including their pets.
34 Wells, 281-282.
35 'New Zealand Settlements Act', 1863, Wells, *Ibid.*, p. 258.
36 Ngata, p. 15.

V - Aggression Without Guns

It was against this background of bloodshed, arising primarily from Maori tribal disputes that, soon after the enervating Taranaki Land War, Te Whiti emerged as the new Maori messiah, with his strategy of 'passive resistance'.

Te Whiti is said to have decided on his course when observing the deaths of the Maori followers of the Hau Hau religion, under another self-styled Prophet, Te Ua Haumene, who stormed Sentry Hill on 30 April 1864, his followers raising their right hands in the belief that God would protect them from bullets. It becomes apparent however that resistance under Te Whiti assumed other forms that were intended to be devastating to the hard-pressed settlers. Others of unquestionably violent nature such as Titokowaru and his cannibal followers joined Te Whiti *en masse* as a change of tactics; not because they had suddenly seen the Godly light of peace and love.

So far from the Administration being intransigent and tyrannical, every effort was made to negotiate with Te Whiti and resolve conflict. Rather, it was Te Whiti and his deputy Tohu who would not negotiate. In 1880 the Government attempted to communicate with Te Whiti in regard to grievances, 'to inquire into any grounds which might exist for discontent among the Natives on the West Coast, and generally into the Native difficulties there'. The report to Governor Sir Arthur Gordon, in regard to the recommendation of the commissioners to seek dialogue, states that the suggestion was met with contempt by Tohu, who threw the written offer back at the Government interpreter:

The Act of last Session, by which Parliament empowered

the Government to give effect to the Commissioners' recommendations, was translated into Maori, and a Government Interpreter was sent to Parihaka to distribute a number of printed copies. He found great difficulty in his attempts to do this, and eventually the copies were thrown back at him by Tohu, who is a sort of brother-prophet, and Te Whiti's principal assistant.[1]

However, Te Whiti stated that he would be willing to see the Governor, the attitude of the administration being that 'no reasonable means for arriving at a satisfactory settlement of those difficulties should be left untried'.[2] Gordon wrote to Te Whiti inviting him to Wellington, or alternatively the Governor would visit Te Whiti at New Plymouth:

I am told that you are desirous of seeing me, and representing to me your view of what should be done to promote this good end. That is very good: and if you will let me know when you will come to Wellington to see me, you shall be received with fitting hospitality, and I will not only listen to whatever you wish to say to me, but also, if you show that wrong has been done, will do justice, in accordance with the law and the will of the Queen.[3]

Parris, the long-serving District Commissioner, was instructed to attend the November 1880 gathering at Parihaka, the claim having been made that Te Whiti was unaware of the Government's intentions. Te Whiti nonetheless prevented Parris from speaking there. Te Whiti's attitude was typical of a cult leader in not wanting his followers to have access to information from the outside world. Parris reported to the Premier that Te Whiti 'unmistakably indicated that he would not treat with any subordinate of the Government, and, consequently, would not

1   Hall, pp. 20-27.
2   *Ibid.*
3   Gov. Sir Arthur Gordon to Te Whiti, Sub-Enclosure 1 to Enclosure 1 in No. 38, Memorandum, in Hall, *Ibid.*

allow me to make any statement'.[4] Te Whiti's megalomania seems to have been of more importance than a settlement with the Government.

Capt. Louis F Knollys was assigned to deliver the invitation of the Governor to Te Whiti. He was left waiting for five hours while Te Whiti played draughts. Part of the Governor's letter was read to Te Whiti who interrupted, stating that he was not interested in discussions, and refused to listen further. Knollys remarked that Te Whiti's habit was to turn his back whenever Knollys talked with him, not replying to Knollys' assertion that the Governor merely wanted to discuss grievances and to find a solution. The following day Knollys sent a message to Te Whiti stating:

> The Governor has recently arrived here, and seeks to settle justly the difficulties. If wrong comes to Te Whiti's people because of the Governor's ignorance of their desires, the evil will have been brought by Te Whiti, because he will not come to make things plain to him.[5]

Knollys visited Te Whiti again and, while more amiable, the messiah would not concede to negotiating. Knollys formed an interesting impression of Te Whiti, being that it was not in Te Whiti's interests for there to be any settlement with the Government, stating:

> The peculiar position in which he is placed, and his own cunning self-complacency, fanaticism, and action with the Government, have won him a share of power and importance far above what he is entitled to by birth or inheritance, and which a satisfactory settlement might considerably endanger.

---

4   R Parris to the Hon, Premier, November 19, 1880, Sub-Enclosure 2 to Enclosure 1 in
     No. 38, Memorandum, in Hall, *Ibid.*
5   Capt. Knollys to His Excellency the Governor, Enclosure 2 in No. 38, Memorandum,
     Hall, op. cit., December 31 1880.

He lives now, seeking, with Tohu and ten others, for the 'truth' - as he considers his present religion, founded on his rendering of the Bible - prophesying and receiving worship; feared by others for his divine attributes and power of witchcraft, and believed in, I think, by himself. This is, to him, a state of happiness, which might be modified were he only to become a contented Maori chief.

That the belief in him is somewhat on the wane I think there is little doubt. Events have not always turned out as he prophesied, in spite of his crafty translations of his prophecies. Those who brought clothes for their deceased relatives, who, he had promised, should rise from the dead, took them home unused, hardly satisfied with the explanation that the prophet had meant the General Resurrection at the last; and some other such failures of his prophecies have raised doubts. But, though belief in him is waning, fear of his supernatural powers of witchcraft is, I fancy, as strong as ever. This waning of the Natives' belief in Te Whiti is, I think, certainly a great inducement to carry on things deliberately, without forcing a collision...[6]

Capt. Knollys was suggesting a scenario in accord with what is now known of cult leaders, as well as of dictators who retain power by perpetual 'states of emergency'; that of a manufactured persecution or danger from the 'outside world', from which the cult or political leader's adherents must withdraw.

One reason that Te Whiti was adamant about not visiting the Governor in Wellington seems to have been part of a contrivance to fulfil a 'prophecy', *The Star* commenting in 1880:

Te Whiti has ingeniously turned the road making and telegraph erection into a fulfilment of his prophesy that the Governor could come to him. He tells the Natives that the

---

6   *Ibid.* Knollys was endorsing the policy urged by many, of doing nothing against Te Whiti, of 'waiting things out', while the settlers suffered.

wire is being brought to Parihaka so that they can talk with the Governor, and therefore the Governor was coming to him as he prophesied years ago.[7]

Previously Te Whiti had prophesied that the road would never be completed. Now he was stating that it would be constructed according to his own divine plan.

Squabbling

Disputes were not only with Pakeha settlers however. A four-year dispute with other Maori over ownership of 100 acres of land at Pihama[8] required police intervention in 1895, and again in 1897 after threats to burn down *whare*.[9] This dispute happened to be between followers of Te Whiti and those of Tohu. In 1895 followers of Te Whiti had planted the land in potatoes at the time that it had been awarded to Tohu. Tohu allowed the Whiti-ites to dig up the potatoes. However, the following year the Whiti-ites took down the gates and entered the property with the intention of cultivating it, resulting in Tohu calling on Constable Twomey to evict the trespassers.[10] In 1897 much damage was done to property when the two factions had come into conflict while cropping. A leader of the Tohu faction who owned 87 of the 100 acres of the land granted by the Native Land Court, laid the information for the arrest of three followers of Te Whiti for wilful damage.[11] Ninety-one chains of fencing had been destroyed, valued at £45 10s, and the threat was made to burn the woman owner's house.[12]

7   Star, Hawera, p. 3.
8   'Native Land Dispute at Pihama. Question of Ownership', *Hawera & Normanby Star*, Volume XXXIII, Issue 3371, 13 October 1896, p. 2.
9   'A Native Dispute', *Thames Star*, Volume XXIX, Issue 8780, 9 September 1897, p. 4.
10   'Native Land Dispute at Pihama. Question of Ownership', *Hawera & Normanby Star*, 1896, p. 2, op. cit.
11   'The Native Land Dispute At Pihama', *Taranaki Herald*, Volume XLVI, Issue 11027, 18 September 1897, p. 2.
12   'The Land dispute at Pihama', *Taranaki Herald*, Volume XLVI, Issue 11029, 21 September 1897, p. 2.

It seems that Pakeha law and even the evil Constabulary, supposedly the syphilitic rapists and looters of Bryce's 1881 raid, were acceptable when the rival Whiti-ites and Tohu-ites were in dispute over the same 'piece of land'. It was precisely such contentions over land ownership between Maori that resulted not only in the frequent scamming of Pakeha buyers by disputed 'owners', but in the genocidal warfare between Maori tribes that was only settled by the enforcement of Pakeha law – at Maori request. As most New Zealanders know, the factionalism and counter-claims among Maori have still not been resolved.

VI - Paradise Lost

The depiction of Parihaka by orthodox academe and other commentators who have sought to continue the cult into the present, is that of a well-ordered, clean, planned, 'modern' community of utopian proportions. The reality was quite different. Parihaka through much of its history was disease-ridden and filthy.

An 1875 report refers to seventy cases of measles resulting in deaths aggravated by the practise by 'native doctors' of putting sufferers into cold water. 'There is a great deal of sickness among the natives, many being troubled with inflammation of the lungs', a contemporary report stated. The deaths ceased after Dr O'Carroll arrived.[1]

In 1879 fever broke out in Parihaka, although no efforts ever seemed to have been made to prevent the free movement of the Maori to and from Parihaka, through colonial settlements. The settlers lived in continual 'unease' as to the possibility of contagion being spread from Parihaka. During that year's fever 'upward of seventy natives' reportedly died.[2] However Te Whiti's followers remained 'emphatic as ever that Te Whiti will bring them to life again',[3] while others had apparently lost faith in Te Whiti's ability to heal and stated that they would not return while sickness prevailed.[4]

1   'The Parihaka Meeting', *Taranaki Herald*, Volume XXIII, Issue 2343, 22 September 1875, p. 2.
2   'Te Whiti's People Leaving on Account of Sickness', *Wanganui Herald*, Volume XII, Issue 3542, 21 October 1879, p. 2.
3   'Patea', *Thames Star*, Volume X, Issue 3380, 22 October 1879, p. 2.
4   'Te Whiti's People Leaving on Account of Sickness', *Wanganui Herald*, op. cit.

By early 1881 Parihaka was reportedly in a poor state with scarcity of food, compelling the digging up of half-ripened potatoes, and many were returning to their own settlements.[5] *The Taranaki Herald* reported that Parihaka was infected by vermin for lack of cleanliness and by overcrowding, that it was 'absolutely filthy through lack of sanitary precautions', and an outbreak of pestilence was feared that summer. The Maori of surrounding communities had neglected their own affairs, and spent much of the time in Parihaka due to the frequency of the gatherings.[6]

In 1884 an outbreak of cellular erysipelas occurred. The Government sent a doctor, and medical supplies, an action for which Te Whiti and Tohu thanked the Native Minister. Dr O'Carroll reported a 'terrible state of filth' there.[7] Further reports stated that the form of erysipelas was known as 'hospital gangrene' and was particularly virulent and contagious:

> Dr O'Carroll worked vigorously and patiently attending the patients all day. In many cases the face, legs, arms, and, indeed, all parts of the body were greatly swollen, and the incisions allowed the pus or matter to escape, thus affording great relief. Great care has to be exercised in operating in this way, as if the poison which escapes from these swellings were to come in contact with the least scratch on the finger or hand of another person, the disease would be at once transmitted...[8]

A newspaper account more descriptive than others states:

---

5   'The State of Affairs at Parihaka', *Wanganui Herald*, Volume XV, Issue 4040, 6 January 1881, p. 2.

6   'The State of Parihaka', *Taranaki Herald*, Volume XXIX, Issue 3836, 12 September 1881, p. 2

7   'Disease at Parihaka', *Marlborough Express*, Volume XX, Issue 340, 23 October 1884, p. 2.

8   'Erysipelas at Parihaka', *Hawera & Normanby Star*, Volume V, Issue 935, 23 October 1884, p. 2

Dr O'Carroll says he never saw the pah dirtier, the human,
pig and dog excrement being up to one's instep all around.
He adds that he never saw such sights in his life, and some
portions of the report are too shocking to quote. Women are
to be seen with their breasts eaten away with the disease,
which is of a very contagious character... [9]

Dr O'Carroll commented that now the situation had been
explained to Te Whiti, who was grateful to the evil Pakeha
Government for sending assistance, he 'takes the necessary steps
to stay the disease'.[10] It was reported that Te Whiti had agreed to
have the Parihaka settlement cleaned up to stamp out erysipelas,
'which has been prevalent there for some time'.[11]

Yet, earlier in the same year other visitors were remarking on the
cleanliness of Parihaka, and its European methods of hygiene
and housing are the images that have come to dominate the
descriptions of the settlement to the exclusion of others. Some
disaffected older Maori remarked on the Pakeha manners Te Whiti
had adopted on his return from Government detention, despite
the claim that he could not be bought. The explanation might be
found in Te Whiti wanting to present a pristine impression of
Parihaka to the Pakeha visitors who often came to participate in
the huge and frequent feasts, which would showcase to Pakeha
Te Whiti's domain. In March 1884 a 'great feast day' was held
involving 100 Pakeha and 1000 Maori. Meals were served with
all the accoutrements of Pakeha civilisation, with the most
extravagant of foods, including plum puddings and various
wines and beer. Waiters served the tables in European style, with
towels slung across their shoulders. The press reporter described
a perplexing occurrence:

9 'Serious Disease at Parihaka', Otago Daily Times, Issue 7093, 7 November 1884, p. 1.
10 'Shocking State of Affairs in Parihaka', Bruce Herald, Volume XVII, Issue 1653, 24
October 1884, p. 3.
11 'Parihaka Natives Taking Dr O'Carroll's Advice', *Poverty Bay Herald*, Volume XI,
Issue 4144, 18 November 1884, p. 2.

There was a procession of about twenty women, dressed in European clothes. For the privilege of exhibiting their figures and dresses, they had to contribute some silver as they entered Te Whiti's house; but to what purpose the money was devoted did not transpire. Tohu, who was dressed in European costume, addressed a few words to them, denouncing extravagance in dress, one of the women replying.[12]

Why were these women in procession at the festivity, and why were they required to pay Te Whiti for the privilege? They drew the ire of Te Whiti's rival, Tohu. Were they prostitutes? At least, it is a mark of Te Whiti's seeking to profit from his own people that the women had to 'contribute some silver' to parade in his house.

The reporter commented that, 'Everything was scrupulously clean, so far as the food was concerned, and the pah was much cleaner than it used to be'.[13] Like Jim Jones who sought to impress the delegation headed by Congressman Ryan at Jonestown, were Pakeha guests often duped? Was Te Whiti a pimp, in addition to being a 'sly grog' seller? Does whore-mongering offer the real explanation for widespread syphilis in Parihaka rather than as a by-product of the Bryce occupation?

Jean Jackson, Ngai Tahu historian, has her own suspicions regarding prostitution at Parihaka: 'The whiff of prostitution and liaisons of Maori soldiers from outside tribes, etc., including non-Maori, with Maori or White women alarmed Government'.[14]

In 1887 a measles epidemic broke out at Parihaka, resulting in deaths, again causing consternation among the settlers through whose towns the Maori travelled on their way to and from

---

12   'Festivities at Parihaka', Star, Issue 4954, 19 March 1884, p. 4.
13   'Festivities at Parihaka', Star, Ibid.
14   Jean Jackson, op. cit.

Parihaka.[15] Naturally, it was the responsibility of the health authorities, under Dr O'Carroll, to provide medication, which was again accepted by Te Whiti. Something of the settlers' worry was expressed in letters to the press:

THE EDITOR. Sir, — 'A Parent' enquires in this evening's paper whether typhoid fever patients cannot be prevented from being brought into town from Parihaka? Surely the Board of Health ought to take steps in the matter. If they can prevent disease from being brought by sea into the place, they have similar powers in respect to land imported diseases. The Board of Health seems to be very lax in their duties. If typhoid is bad at Parihaka now, what will it be in the autumn? [16]

'Sly Grog'

In 1893, reporting on the gathering for 18 September, which was said to have been particularly large, and to have been an attempt to revive the old enthusiasm, 'dark sayings were again resorted to'. The meeting was noted for its fervour through the use of 'intoxicative drinks'.[17] However, in 1880 Captain Knollys had reported that Te Whiti prohibited the use alcohol at Parihaka, [18] while the Governor, Sir Arthur Gordon, reported that wherever Te Whiti's influence reigns 'drunkenness is unknown'.[19] This is clearly incorrect, and is indicative that Government officials, far from being antagonistic towards Te Whiti, saw him in a more positive light than he merited.

---

15 'An Epidemic Amongst the Natives', *Wanganui Chronicle*, Volume XXX, Issue 11527, 4 July 1887, p. 2.
16 'Typhoid Fever', *Taranaki Herald*, Volume XXX, Issue 3954, 31 January 1882, p. 2.
17 'Te Whiti's Tomfoolery. Large Meeting at Parihaka', Bush Advocate, Volume XI, Issue 838, 30 September 1893, p. 3.
18 G W Rusden, Aureretanga: Groans of the Maoris, op. cit., p. 87.
19 G W Rusden, *Ibid.*, p. 86. As will be related, Sir Arthur was later involved in a libel suit bought by Bryce against Rusden, the Governor having given Rusden false information about Bryce.

Neither does the supposed sobriety of the Parihakians accord with the prosecutions for 'sly grog selling'. In 1894 a press report was carried of an account at Parihaka that focuses on the alcohol and in particular the manner by which Te Whiti was scamming his followers with the incessant banquets, where the food was provided by his followers who then had to pay for the honour of eating it. The report is worth reproducing in its entirety:

The *Hawera Star*, a paper which is as a rule very ably conducted, and in whose statements confidence is put by a large number of readers along the west coast of the North Island, published last week a most remarkable article upon the subject of the famous Maori settlement of Parihaka and of the chiefs who are at the head of a movement which, if correctly described by the paper in question, should certainly attract the notice of the Government with a view to steps being taken by the proper authorities to bring about its speedy discontinuance.

The recent arrests for sly grog selling at the famous native settlement have, it appears, directed the attention of the *Star* writer to the system in vogue at Parihaka, and the results of the enquiries that he has made are certainly most sensational in their character. From the *Star* account it appears that the periodical meetings at night at the *pah* are simply scenes of drunkenness and unbridled immorality, largely contributed to of course by the vile liquor sold by the grog-shop keepers. 'A well-known chief in the Hawera district,' says the *Star*, 'was so impressed with the danger with which such scenes — as those witnessed nightly at Parihaka during meetings are frequent — that he made representation to Tohu, his titular leader, with the result that Tohu commanded that all who acknowledged his sway should cease from selling liquor lest trouble arise between the Maoris and persons who go to Parihaka to take part in the orgies. It must be premised that the tribes south of Parihaka owe allegiance to Tohu, whilst those north of

that place regard Te Whiti as their prophet and leader. Te
Whiti, it is said, issued no command for the cessation of
grog-selling, hence those arrested for that offence were his
followers.'

The Hawera journalist next proceeds to deal with the disposition
of the large sums which from time to time have been contributed
to Te Whiti and Tohu for one purpose or another, but which,
according to him, are seized and held as the purely private
property of the two chiefs mentioned and of a little coterie of
devoted followers who may vulgarly said to be 'in the swim'.

'The whole machinery at the command of the two false
prophets is put in motion for the collection of money,
which is hoarded or expended on the building of houses,
which, when used as eating-houses, become themselves
reproductive, and further add to the hoard. For what
purpose this money is intended has never been divulged,
but the system is on a par with the Liberator Building
Society in swindling, and the cloak of religion is thrown
around the collection of funds, only in this instance the
religion is of a more materialistic character. Were such
a scheme worked by Europeans the police would be on
the track of the schemers. The accumulation of money at
Parihaka is said to be enormous, comparatively speaking.
It has been stated at £80,000, and a venturesome guess at
£50,000 was immediately condemned as too low, though
we confess we do not know on what data. It is untold gold
and uncounted notes, no account being kept by those who
have charge of it— two natives appointed by Te Whiti and
Tohu. The gold, it is said, is kept in bulk, the notes in 50lbs
flour bags.'

It has been very commonly supposed by visitors to Parihaka,
and by the public generally, that the large sums of money given
to the chiefs have been spent by them on the big 'gorges' which
periodically take place at the settlement, but it appears that these

banquets are not only self-supporting, but are indeed made a source of further revenue by the wily little ring who so cleverly exploit the ignorance and fanaticism of their less *oute* followers. *The Star* says on this head: —

'It must not be supposed that the periodical feasts, almost monthly in their incidence, are a charge on the bank, on the contrary each one adds more and more to the hoard. The meals are served in European style in the large weather-board eating-houses. A receptacle for coin is placed at intervals down every table, and each is expected to contribute who partakes. It would appear to be a test of chieftainship; the more a native gives the more distinguished is his rank: hence the plutocrat among the aboriginals will haughtily toss his £5 into the glass, whilst the *tutua* humbly insinuates his lowly shilling into the same receptacle. It was asked if the collection equals the expenditure at each gathering, and it was generally agreed that there must be a large surplus. It was explained that most of the food was supplied by the natives themselves, who gave it to Tohu and Te Whiti in bulk, that these chiefs had it cooked, and placed on the tables in the eating-house, and the donors were then practically charged so much a meal for their own food, and a nice little chieftainship thrown in as an incentive for the disbursement of more cash. Again, in the building of the eating-houses the timber is generally found[20] by the natives, who hand it to Te Whiti and Tohu, who then have the carpenters to pay out of their accumulations.'

Our contemporary proceeds to point out that the effect of the system which it has now shown up is to make the natives along the coast idle and vicious, but it cannot see any clear and easy remedy for the state of things it has unfolded. The false pretences of the prophets are implied in ambiguous language,

---

20   'Found' is an interesting euphemism to use. The Parihaka Maori stole wood from the hapless Pakeha settlers.

and so complete is the fanatical hold these men have over the natives, that it is very questionable, the *Star* thinks, whether any of their followers could be persuaded to give such evidence as would justify the Government in active interference. As to the result of the system, its evils cannot well be enumerated:

'There is probably not one of all those who contribute to the funds at Parihaka who knows what is to become of this money. The fruits of all their industry in grass seed threshing and fungus picking, goes there *in globo*, part of the proceeds of sales of land are taken in bulk, and part of the half yearly rents received from the Public Trustee are either handed over to the prophets or expended in the grog shops, or gambled away in the billiard room at Parihaka. Truly Parihaka is a menace to the advancement of the Maori, and the prophets a festering sore on the body of the native race'.

It is to be hoped that the attention of the Government will be drawn to the article from which we have quoted, and that it may be found possible, assuming the *Star's* account to be true, to put an end to the highly scandalous state of affairs which, *pace* our Hawera contemporary, prevails at the present time at Parihaka.[21]

Rev. A W H Compton of the Anglican Church provided an interesting account of Parihaka in 1899, which accords with the previous account:

Parihaka and the conditions of life there are described by the Rev A. W. H. Compton as follows: 'From one point of view, that of the great influence of Te Whiti and Tohu, the Native dress and customs, the Natives' meetings and their dances, it was interesting and picturesque; but it had a terribly dark side. It was a hindrance to religious progress,

---

21 'The Truth About Parihaka', *Marlborough Express*, Volume XXX, Issue 33, 8 February 1894, p. 2.

for it was a nest of vice, and a hotbed of immorality. There was no licensed house there, but there were two drinking saloons, there was constant drunkenness, and things went on which he could only hint at. Apart from its moral evil Parihaka was a tax on the Natives financially. Most of them were poor and their resources were terribly drained by the demands made on them for the monthly meetings.' This is the kind of place, says the *Hawera Star*, which is bracketed by some papers with Te Aute College as a means of uplifting the Maoris.[22]

Yet another account, the same year, comes from a Taranaki Maori who had spent four years at Te Aute Native College. He visited Parihaka and wrote of what he saw. He observed widespread gambling, and also noted two houses where alcohol was sold in large quantities daily, with Maori expending much of their money:

It is impossible for me to describe the scenes of drunkenness and immorality that are enacted in these two places at times. The liquor supplied is not, I am assured, of the best quality, and after it has passed through the hands of the Maori retailer it is little better than rank poison. I think that this state of things is well known to the authorities, as the beer-saloon keeper has been summoned several times, but without visible effect on his trade.[23]

The beer seller referred to as having been summoned by the authorities several times for 'sly grog selling', is likely to have been Te Whetu, one of Te Whiti's chief advisers, who had a history of resisting arrest, and who had been suspected of murder years previously but was never tried. It seems that a good living could be made by some Maori from their brethren by providing the services of alcohol and gambling, and other services only hinted at.

22 'Parihaka', Star, Issue 6528, 4 July 1899, p. 1.
23 'Parihaka and its Vices', *Otago Witness*, Issue 2342, 19 January 1899, p. 12.

VI - Paradise Lost

As for the medical conditions that had been long maintained by Dr O'Carroll, by 1902 the benefits of Pakeha medicine seem to have been neglected, as there was no prohibition against unqualified practitioners, with Parihaka having become 'a happy hunting ground for the quacks', since if a patient died nothing was heard about it.[24] This presumably referred to 'Maori traditional medicine', which is again being practised at the present-day Parihaka 'peace festivals', in addition to the traditional (?) practice of pot smoking.[25]

Authorities closed two 'sly grog' shops in 1898.[26] The prophet himself could hardly have disapproved of the sales: In 1887 Te Whiti had been fined £10 for 'sly grog selling'.[27] When a force under Inspector Pardy came to arrest Te Whiti's confidante, Te Whetu, for 'sly grog selling' 'a general rush was made [at the constables], constable Twomey being thrown to the ground and constable Roche also got a severe handling'. The affray lasted around 15 to 20 minutes, and was brought under control by the order to fix bayonets. Apparently this is an acceptable part of 'passive resistance' because it did not involve the use of guns by Maori. Te Whetu was known as 'Te Whiti's fighting man' and was considered a 'notorious character'.[28] In 1895 Wehi was also convicted on two charges of 'sly grog selling' at Parihaka.[29]

According to Jean Jackson, a Botanist who has studied the use of plants by Maori, Parihaka women were put to work making corn liquor, and she suspects that Te Whiti kept his followers drugged:

24 'The Parihaka Prophet', *Otago Witness*, Issue 2546, 31 December 1902, p. 54.
25 Refer to 'Conclusion' for accounts of the 2009 festival.
26 'Raid on Sly Grog Shops. A haul at Parihaka', *Nelson Evening Mail*, Volume XXXII, Issue XXXII, 13 October 1898, p. 3.
27 'Not a Prophet in his own country', *Grey River Argus*, Volume XXXV, Issue 5958, 28 July 1887, p. 2. *Bay Of Plenty Times*, Volume XV, Issue 2170, 1 August 1887, p. 2.
28 'Skirmish at Parihaka', Northern Advocate, 6 August 1887, p. 3.
29 'Parihaka Sly Grog Selling', *Evening Post*, Volume L, Issue 151, 24 December 1895, p. 2.

Often women had to steep corn in pools to make liquor or others drank liquids 'the prophet' never paid a licence for. I suspected that 'peace' came at times from native sedatives, a karaka or kaua kaua infusion - the Hau Hau might have used exciters, magic mushroom or pukatea. (It has properties like mainline drugs). Or mixtures. It leads to an idea that may explain odd streams of superior thoughts...[30]

Mrs Jackson wondered why many Maori have birth defects, such as her own 'slight tribal mutation of the thumbs'. 'A toxic staple food could damage the race. Fernroot. What about Parihaka? Did Te Whiti sedate his people at all? And when so many of the Hau Hau came to reside, after the cannibal rituals mixed with Catholic religion, had ugly events from the 'fifties or 'sixties returned?'[31] Jackson states of 'corn liquor' that it was made in New Zealand the same way it is still made in Africa. As a Botanist, she states:

It has a harmful effect on the human body's immunity, if it doesn't also affect genetic inheritance (mutation), cause blindness, insanity - or death. Taken alongside tribal drugs, or maybe with other types of alcohol, South Africa's medical authorities noted new forms of religion or aberrations and all manner of ideas involving politics or witchcraft could be found not only in tribal villages but in towns.[32]

The use of toxic drugs and corn liquor among Te Whiti's followers, Mrs Jackson suggests, might account at least in part for the mass religious delusions that were a feature of the settlement.

While Te Whiti and his cohorts were profiting from the selling of illicit alcohol, which reports claim were toxic, to his people,

30   Jean Jackson, op. cit.
31   *Ibid.*
32   *Ibid.*

drinking was a matter of serious concern for those who had a genuine regard for the Maori. The Women's Christian Temperance Union, comprising 1,497 members, included 252 Maori, and worked hard to counter alcohol consumption among the Maori.[33] In 1907, the year of the deaths of both Te Whiti and Tohu, the Native Land Commission added their concern about the consumption of alcohol, describing this as a 'great evil [that] has worked great havoc amongst the Maori people':

...There is often found a breaking-out of credulity which takes the form of following some tohunga, or prophet. Sanitary measures are often neglected, though a great improvement has taken place in recent years in this connection. Further, there is a thriftlessness, or a want of care of money earned, or obtained from the sale of land, that is appalling. Such thriftlessness means that the money was wasted in ways that tend to the physical, moral, and intellectual deterioration of the race, and the sale of land by the Maoris is not only in many instances leaving them landless, but is killing them...[34]

The description is applicable to the Parihaka cult in every respect.

In 1916 Sir Robert Stout, jurist and Premier, warned that alcohol would destroy the Maori race, stating, 'it would be a great pity if such a fine race as the Maoris were to pass away', as the Tasmanian natives had through rampant alcoholism.[35] Such widespread concern for the welfare of the Maori expressed throughout all sections of Pakeha society stands in contrast to the image that is conveyed today of the ruthless and exploitive colonialists.

33　'Napier', North Otago Times, Volume XXXVI, Issue 9141, 2 March 1898, p. 3.
34　'Future of the Maori', Evils to be Combated', Poverty Bay Herald, Volume XXXIV, Issue 11131, 2 August 1907, p. 4.
35　'Maoris and Drunkenness. Appeal by Sir Robert Stout', Poverty Bay Herald, Volume XLIII, Issue 14100, 18 September 1916, p. 2.

VII - 'Passive but Bounceable'

The emphasis on the 'passive resistance' of Te Whiti and his Parihaka community is now legendary, with comparisons being made to other modern liberal icons such as Mandela, Gandhi and Martin Luther King. However, the Parihaka cult was intended to be as ruinous to the livelihood of settlers as any call to arms. Buildings on private holdings were continually vandalised and settlers' property ploughed up.

Republic of Hawera

In 1879 12 Maori returning from Parihaka entered Loveridge's Store, Oakura, and pulled stock off the shelves. 'They were very bounceable', and the Armed Constabulary ejected them,[1] although they do not seem to have been detained. Such was the exasperation of the Pakeha settlers at the destruction of their property, while the Government vacillated, that in 1879 they formed the Republic of Hawera and elected James Livingston J.P., a veteran of the Taranaki War, as president, his property having been a particular target of Te Whiti's and Titokowaru's followers.[2] Locals organised themselves as the Hawera Rifles to patrol the area until the Government could be persuaded to send the Armed Constabulary.[3]

Daily Vandalism

Horses were reported stolen from the Quinlivan property by Parihaka Maori, who refused to return them.[4] Te Whiti's followers

---

1   'The Native Difficulty', *Wanganui Chronicle*, Volume XXI, Issue 4077, 25 June 1879, p. 2.
2   Livingston and his wife had been forced to flee their farm when Titokowaru was running rampant. His warriors took what sheep and cattle they could and slaughtered the rest. 'An Eventful Life', Colonist, Volume LIII, Issue 13109, 18 May 1911, p. 4.
3   'Excitement at Hawera', *Poverty Bay Herald*, Volume VI, Issue 818, 25 June 1879, p. 2.
4   'The Native Embroglio', *Waikato Times,* Volume XV, Issue 1281, 14 Sep 1880, p. 3.

also attempted to extort a 20 shilling toll from travellers under threat of being brought before Te Whiti at Parihaka.[5]

Much of the activity involved Te Whiti's followers continually fencing lands, plough up settlers' property, vandalism, theft, and pulling out surveying pegs, with daily arrests ensuing. Te Whiti aimed to maintain this until continual arrests became a burden on the Government. A lenient policy by the Constabulary of immediately releasing those arrested was attempted, but Te Whiti's followers kept returning. When the Constabulary posted a strong guard in an area following arrests, preventing the return of the Maori the following day, 'they then became frantic and very violent, insisting on either being arrested or else allowed to go on fencing'. Te Whiti then sent a message that unless they were arrested, twice as many would be sent back the following day, after which the group was detained.[6] Te Whiti had stated that he would send all his men, women and children to prison, rather than negotiate, describing himself as 'only an agent' of the divine, as foretold in prophecies of the coming of 'a great person... to settle all things'.[7]

A newly built stockyard was pulled down on a property at Ngakumikum by Maori from Parihaka in 1881. The belligerent attitude among the Parihaka Maori was notable.[8] In 1883 a newspaper report commented:

About two hundred natives, en route to Parihaka, passed through town this morning. About thirty of the natives who offered violence to Mr. Hursthouse were amongst them. The natives intend to be present at a tangi at Oakura today,

5   'News From the Camp', *Taranaki Herald*, Volume XXVIII, Issue 3583, 4 Nov1880, p. 2.

6   'Native Affairs Opposite Parihaka', *Evening Post*, Volume XX, Issue 192, 18 August 1880, p. 2.

7   'Letter from Parihaka', *Hawera & Normanby Star*, Volume I, Issue 38, 21 August 1880, p. 2.

8   'The Parihaka Settlement', *Grey River Argus*, Volume XXIV, Issue 4070, 14 September 1881, p. 2

and then proceed to Parihaka. Amongst the natives are some of the worst of the late disturbers of the peace. The natives say that they will go to Parihaka, and nothing shall stop them.[9]

In 1885 Parihaka Maori were still destroying property, and the settlers were in a constant state of distress. A cottage owned by a settler, Plummer, had its windows and doors removed. When credit was stopped by the owner of a premises, the Maori dismantled and removed to Parihaka in its entirety the building that had been used as a billiard hall. [10] That year timber was removed from the property of Mr Robson, with which he intended building a cabin, the intention of the thieves being to remove it to Parihaka.[11]

In 1886 Te Whiti with nine Maori appeared at Court on charges of forcibly entering the property of Mr Hastie. Evidence was given by Te Whetu, Te Whiti's chief adviser, that Te Whiti had given him the order to plough settlers' land at Oakura at the same time.[12] At Inaha, Titokowaru led 400 Maori on to the Hastie farm, with a large amount of building material, and had erected a tent and large heaps of firewood, 'prepared for a permanent stay'. They proceeded to erect a large *whare*, after having released their horses and bullocks onto the farm.[13] One again one is struck, on reading this account, by the newspaper's sympathy for Parihaka hooligans who were attempting to wreck a farmer's livelihood, rather than for the Pakeha who were deputised to assist the outnumbered Constabulary. Despite the assumptions of today about supposedly anti-Maori and 'racist' attitudes towards the Maori in colonial times, the press even in those times was often as biased against the whites as it is now.

---

9   *Hawera & Normanby Star*, Volume IV, Issue 584, August 29 1883, p. 2.
10   'Troublesome Natives at Parihaka', *Marlborough Express*, Volume XXI, Issue 93, 27 April 1885, p. 2.
11   'More Maori Troubles', *Hawera & Normanby Star*, Volume VI, Issue 1058, 8 July 1885, p. 2.
12   'The Maori Disturbance', *West Coast Times*, Issue 6275, 23 July 1886, p. 4.
13   'Arrest of Te Whiti', *Te Aroha News*, Vol. IV, Issue 162, 24 July 1886, p. 8.

In 1887 three Maori resisted arrest, and were fined, and one, Te Aroa, who had 'assaulted the police', received three months hard labour in what seems to have been a lenient punishment for the nature of the offence.[14] In 1897 a brawl was reported between a part–Maori farmer and Parihaka 'pacifists', when they pulled down a newly erected fence.[15] As late as 1898 returning ex-convicts who had been jailed for ploughing up settlers' land, were being greeted at Parihaka by brass bands and extolled by chiefs 'for their bravery and martyrdom'.[16]

Such incidences indicate the belligerent nature behind the façade of passive resistance that the settlers had to long endure. This belligerence did not stop even after the much-condemned occupation of Parihaka by Bryce's forces and the dispersal of outsiders in 1881, as the above accounts show.

Ploughing the Land

Te Whiti's primary strategy was to plough up the land of European settlers and to fence off land that had been designated for European settlement. District Commissioner Parris stated in his 1882 report:

> The success achieved in the ejectment of the surveyors from the Waimate Plains inflated Te Whiti's vanity, and the faith of his followers in his attainments, and thus led him on to the further aggressive measure of sending out parties of natives to enter upon and plough land of European settlers at seven different places between Hawera and the White Cliffs...[17]

---

14 "The Parihaka affray," *Wanganui Chronicle*, Volume XXX, Issue 11547, 2 August 1887, p. 2.

15 'Parihaka Maoris. Another Fencing Dispute', *Nelson Evening Mail*, Volume XXXI, Issue 253, 25 October 1897, p. 3.

16 'Reception of Liberated Maoris at Parihaka', *Wanganui Chronicle*, Volume XLIII, Issue 15000, 19 July 1898, p. 2.

17 R Parris, 1882, G. 1, No. 10, op. cit.

VII - 'Passive but Bounceable'

About 180 of the offenders were arrested and gaoled. Soon afterward, a Royal Commission recommended that a full investigation be made into Maori grievances with a view to settling disputes. Maori were frequently visited by officers of the Crown to keep them fully informed as to the developments of the surveying, which included the lands reserved for Maori with due regard for burial grounds and fisheries. However, Te Whiti determined that the road being pushed through the district would not be completed, 'prophesying' that the 'two ends would not meet'.[18] This was followed by daily fencing across the road. Parris stated that 'very small children' were sent out for the purpose:

> Occasionally another party composed of over a hundred very small children ... designated the tatarakihi (locusts) were sent out from Parihaka to traverse the road through the cultivation, warbling, like a flock of blight birds, an incantation taught them by Tohu.[19]

Parris mentioned something of the extent and nature of the land reserved for Maori use, and the settlement of Maori who were not part of the Parihaka cult:

> Finding it was useless to expect any concession or compromise from Te Whiti, the Government determined on commencing the survey of the block of land, seaward of the new road, known as the Parihaka Block, for sale and settlement, as recommended by the Royal Commission. All their fishing sites and sacred places were reserved for the natives, and a large reserve on the south bank of

---

18 In a sympathetic article in The *Evening Post*, Wellington, it was claimed that Te Whiti did not make this prophecy, but merely meant that there was a swamp in the way. It is an example of how the colonial press, so far from being universally antagonistic towards Te Whiti, was often willing to give him the benefit of the doubt, perhaps on the basis that the further away the newspaper was from Taranaki, the more charitable it could afford to be. 'Two Blacks Don't Make One White', *Evening Post*, Volume XIX, Issue 116, 20 May 1880, Page 2.

19 R Parris, 1882, G. 1, No. 10, op. cit.

the Kapoaiaio River, containing altogether 714 acres. On the banks of the Waitotoroa River there were extensive clearings, made by natives who had come from distant parts, but did not belong to either Parihaka or the Taranaki District. Five hundred and forty-five acres were reserved from sale for a year or two, in order during that time to prepare them for clearing off, these lands having been mapped as waste lands of the Crown. In addition to this it was intended to make a continuous reserve of 25,000 acres from the Waiwherenui River to the Moutoti River, abutting on the new road on the inland side.[20]

Parris stated that the insinuation by some that the Maori had not been properly informed of what land had been reserved 'is not only unfair but notoriously false', and that Te Whiti himself was fully aware.

Large numbers came out from Parihaka to fence off Government land that was being surveyed for European settlement, greatly outnumbering the Constabulary. Parris stated, 'It was known that they had come to a decision to engage in a hand to hand struggle with the Constabulary'. Rather than engage in conflict, which would have necessitated the Constabulary firing upon their attackers, the Government resolved to avoid any such situation.

Violent Metaphors

Several months before Bryce's occupation of Parihaka, matters were reaching boiling point, although it is part of the myth that all was well and Bryce's move on the settlement was unjust. A major feature of the frequent gatherings at Parihaka was to hear Te Whiti speak his prophetic 'metaphors'. They were deliberately phrased to be enigmatic. In September 1881, Te Whiti addressed the regular assembly in a particularly infamous manner, Parris reporting that the speech was phrased,

---

20   *Ibid.*

...in language which, literally interpreted, meant a declaration of war. This caused a state of alarm throughout the district, and the settlers appealed to Government for arms and ammunition, and for the militia to be organised for self-defence. When Te Whiti learnt what the effect of his language had been, he tried to explain it away by stating that what he had said was metaphorical, that the interpreters did not understand him. In fact, no one but himself could understand what he meant to convey to his hearers, and the interpreters were of course in duty bound to furnish a literal interpretation of what he said.[21]

It could be contended that given the volatility of the situation, Te Whiti's speech was a veiled threat couched in the usual messianic language. Parris commented:

For many years past Te Whiti has led his followers on by his prophetical discourses from one device to another, shifting his ground from time to time, until he had exhausted his stock of metaphorical imaginations, and at the September meeting he entertained them with something practical, but very dangerous, which brought things to a climax.[22]

A press report of Te Whiti's speech shows why the settlers would become concerned. Te Whiti's delivery was of a more 'earnest' nature than usual. He stated that matters had now changed. He did not recognise the Government. He stated that while his followers had been taken prisoner as a result of their obstruction of surveying, they must not allow themselves to be taken again. He concluded:

If the Constabulary strike, you must strike them back; if they strike you with a stick, strike them back with a stick; if they fire at you, fire at them. On no account be taken

21 *Ibid.*
22 *Ibid.*

prisoners. Trust in God, and rely on your guns. If there were 10,000 soldiers at Pungarehu – nay 20,000 soldiers there – it would not matter – Pungarehu would only be a grave for them. [23]

Tohu next spoke, and applauded Te Whiti's words. Noticing someone taking notes, he stated:

We have done with writing and with talking now. We have had it long enough and the days have come when we must act…. We have done with ploughing and fencing. There are two tribes opposed to each other. The big tribe are the Europeans and the small tribes are the Maoris…. The bubble has burst and this is our time for action. I agree with Te Whiti that we must trust in god and rely on our guns…. If the Constabulary wrestle with you, then you must wrestle with them; if they fire upon you, you must fire upon them, and I will be with you.[24]

If the press and others had misinterpreted Te Whiti's metaphorical speech, then so did Tohu. Subsequent claims as to misinterpretation are disingenuous and the responsibility must rest with Te Whiti if his intentions were misunderstood. It is more likely that he intended to be interpreted in that manner to force a confrontation, and thereby fulfil his prophecies of martyr status, while maintaining his image as a wronged peacemaker. The *Herald* correspondent reported his impressions that the gathering was not so 'pacific' in nature as previously, and that the attitude towards strangers was not amiable. The correspondent wrote that Te Whiti stated of himself, 'I am the land, and the people are in my hand'. He made the situation analogous to Israel:

---

23   'Parihaka Meeting. Te Whiti and Tohu's Speeches. Te Whiti defies the Government. Affairs look Serious', *Taranaki Herald*, Volume XXIX, Issue 3842, 19 September 1881, p. 2.
24   *Ibid.*

The peace that existed had passed away – there is no peace now. You have tried to keep the peace, but were not allowed. There will be no teaching today, for all is trouble around me, and all the talk will be of fighting, for nothing but fighting will put what is wrong right. ... The evil of the world is now loose among us, and there is nothing to stop it now but fighting. Let the Government and the King and the people listen to the words of this meeting; let them take heed what I say; let them depart from the land; let them cease to bring their evil to us... Go – go all of you, and look upon me as your protector. Take your arms and the blessing of the Atua[25] will be with you.[26]

Te Whiti and Tohu referred to the coming *pakanga*[27] and made Biblical references to the sufferings of the prophets and the apostles. Tohu stated that the previous obstructive tactics would end, and fighting would begin. All the prior resistance had been calm before the coming *mate*[28]. Unless the King and the Whites were defeated the Maori would be 'swallowed up'. The fight was for 'all the land'.

It is not I who say this, but the Atua through me, who utters the words...The Atua approves of what we are doing. It comes from him, what I am saying. Things have been quiet for a long time, but that has passed away.... Things are now the same as in the days of the Great Dragon.[29]

While inspecting the area Native Minister Col. Roberts sought the advice of a scholar of Maori, Charles Messenger, who was a Licensed Native Interpreter, regarding Te Whiti's widely reported inflammatory speech, and was assured that it had been translated fairly, 'and in no way exaggerated'.[30] During Te

---

25   God. *Maori Dictionary*, op. cit.
26   'Parihaka Meeting', *Taranaki Herald*, op. cit.
27   Battle, strife, hostility, war. *Maori Dictionary*, op. cit.
28   Be dead, beaten, killed... *Maori Dictionary*, *Ibid*.
29   'Parihaka Meeting', *Taranaki Herald*, op. cit.
30   'Native News', *Hawera & Normanby Star*, Volume II, Issue 152, 28 September 1881, p.

Whiti's trial in November 1881 Charles Messenger was present for cross-examination. He testified he had known Te Whiti for 25 years and had attended many of the gatherings at Parihaka for nine years. He attested to the accuracy of another licensed interpreter who had also been at the September 1881 gathering, Captain Carrington, who had known Te Whiti for 35 years, and who had stated from his notes that Te Whiti had declared in his September speech that it was right that the quarrel should be at Parihaka, telling Maori and Pakeha to bring their guns, as 'fighting alone will settle things at this time'.[31]

Te Whiti's September 1881 speech was the culmination of years of messianic and apocalyptic rhetoric, and was not out of context. In June 1879 Te Whiti had spoken of a vision in which he saw Christ who told him that bullets fired at Maori would return and kill the Pakeha, and that in the event of war Christ would descend and drive the Whites into the sea. He stated that those Maori who did not come to Parihaka would be killed by supernatural means.[32] In the gathering for September 1879 Te Whiti stated that,

> …he was a supreme power on earth, having been invested by the Almighty with supreme authority. If a builder built a house, it would not stand unless he sanctioned it; if a blacksmith welded a piece of iron together, it would not hold unless he caused it to hold together; nor could doctors perform any cures unless his spirit was with them. He was the chief corner stone; all people and tongues are under his sway. He dwelt for a short time on the matter of the arresting of the prisoners. He exonerated the prisoners from all blame, and took all censure and blame in connection with their unlawful proceedings upon himself. He had caused them to be taken prisoners, and he alone could free them from imprisonment.[33]

3.

31 'The State Trials', *Star*, Issue 4233, 15 November 1881, p. 3.
32 'The Native Difficulty, Te Whiti's Vision. Maoris Have Charmed Lives. Europeans Be Driven into the Sea', *Wanganui Chronicle*, Volume XXI, Issue 4069, 16 June 1879, p. 2.
33 'The Parihaka Meeting', *Taranaki Herald*, Volume XXVII, Issue 3231, 19 September

Like all of Te Whiti's reported speeches there was contention as to whether he was misunderstood. Historian Keith Sinclair's opinion, at least on the speech at this September 1879 gathering, was that it had been interpreted correctly, and that R S Thompson was 'an excellent translator'.[34]

In October 1879 Te Whiti called the Government a rata tree and the Members of Parliament bees sucking honey from the rata flower. He stated that he would 'cut down the tree and scatter the bees'.[35] The *Thames Star* commented that despite the persistence in claiming that peace should prevail, the Parihaka Maori were still offering high prices for black powder.[36]

In March 1880 Te Whiti's speech was also interpreted by the press to be of a warlike nature. Yet it would not be correct to think that the colonialist media was universally critical of Te Whiti. On the contrary, then, as now, Parihaka had its partisans in influential Pakeha quarters. It seems to have been the *modus operandi* of Te Whiti to make inflammatory speeches, only to soon afterward claim that he had been misinterpreted and that they were meant as parables and metaphors which only he could interpret.

In 1879 Te Whiti stated of those who had been jailed for ploughing and vandalising settler property that they 'belonged to the holy army of martyrs'.[37] Today, we are more familiar with such inflammatory talk coming from a Muslim in regard to *Jihad* and 'suicide bombers'. In February 1881 at the Parihaka gathering, where recently returned prisoners were present, Te Whiti stated:

> Though a small tribe, they were the greatest of all; and, like the centre pole of the *whare*, they hold up the whole

---

1879, p. 2.

34 K Sinclair, op. cit., pp. 29-30.

35 'Dissensions at Parihaka', *Evening Post*, Volume XVIII, Issue 100, 24 October 1879, p. 2.

36 'Hawera', *Thames Star*, Volume X, Issue 3226, 21 June 1879, p. 2.

37 New Zealand Times, 15 August 1897. Cited by K Sinclair, op. cit., p. 821.

structure of society, as the pole holds up the roof. There was still a time to elapse, but only a short one, before all was completed. The whole was to be finished on the advent of one man, and the land will be returned in the same way as the prisoners.[38]

Just as there were complaints by Te Whiti and others that his infamous September 1881 speech had been misinterpreted, so too the claim was made for his speech in March 1880. Hence, *The Whanganui Chronicle*, in *supporting* Te Whiti, claimed that the reports of his speech had been 'grossly incorrect'. Although *The Chronicle's* own reporter at the March gathering did not know Maori, *The Chronicle* claimed that the interpretation of the speech reported by other newspapers 'bristles with blunders and falsehood and is of no value whatever, except as a record to prove how far some will go astray when they allow themselves to be blinded by party feeling'.[39] Certain newspapers had reported that the speeches of both Te Whiti and Tohu had 'an uncomfortable definiteness' when put in the context of previous statements. They both spoke of war, emphasising that it is a war of Pakeha making, but a war nonetheless that they would pursue when the time was right. Te Whiti challenged: 'If any great European here today says that he can bring a flood on the land, I say to him, "Bring the flood"', adding that because Europeans have plenty of guns 'do not think that you will succeed'. Tohu stated,

> no man shall take the land from us. … I own all the land and all the plantations and will not let them go…. I have constantly said that tomorrow is the day for using guns and the bayonet, and not today.[40]

Replying to the contention by *The Chronicle* that the speeches

---

38   "The Parihaka Meeting," *Hawera & Normanby Star*, Volume I, Issue 89, 19 February 1881, p. 2.
39   Editorial, *Wanganui Chronicle*, Volume XXII, Issue 4287, 24 March 1880, p. 2.
40   'The Taranaki Difficulty', Hawke's Bay Herald, Volume XXI, Issue 5642, 20 March 1880, p. 2.

had been misinterpreted with malice, Thomas McDonnell, who had assisted the *Herald* reporter, stated that he had interpreted the speeches sentence by sentence as they were spoken, both Te Whiti and Tohu speaking slowly and distinctly, and that the speeches had been reported accurately.[41]

The month previous to the inflammatory September 1881 gathering, Te Whiti had prophesied that Pakeha Government would be at an end, and in conjunction with this had alluded to Biblical references of flood and fire that wasted the land.[42] Then in October 1881, despite the volatility of the situation, Te Whiti and Tohu, speaking on the return of 200 released prisoners to Parihaka, stated that resistance would continue no matter how many thousands of Constabulary were sent. 'The walls would fall down. European power would be broken'.[43] The two prophets had continued to use the same rhetoric despite complaining of being misunderstood.

If Te Whiti was genuinely incensed that his speeches were always misinterpreted and that only he could interpret them, why did he not try to speak with plainer meaning, or provide interpretations, since he claimed to be the only individual capable of doing so? Knowing the volatile situation, and the distress his speech in September had caused among the settlers, Te Whiti nonetheless warned the Constabulary that his followers would start the widespread ploughing up of settlers' fields on the Waimate Plains. In September 1881 Titokowaru, the apostle of ritual cannibalism, and about 200 of his people left their settlement with their chattels to resettle in Parihaka.[44]

The entire Colony was expecting war, the Taranaki settlers were

---

41 'Our Reports', *Wanganui Herald*, Volume XII, Issue 3672, 25 March 1880, p. 3.

42 'Te Whiti and the Termination of European Supremacy', *Evening Post*, Volume XXII, Issue 43, 19 August 1881, p. 2.

43 'The Maori Difficulty. The Parihaka Meeting', *Wanganui Herald*, Volume XV, Issue 4496, 17 October 1881, p. 2.

44 'New Plymouth This Day', *Poverty Bay Herald*, Volume VIII, Issue 1437, 28 September 1881, p. 2.

imploring the Government to send assistance and, as Parris puts it: 'Volunteers from all parts of the colony nobly responded when called on to take the field'. These 'noble volunteers', putting their lives on the line with the expectation that they would face armed resistance from religious fanatics who believed like the *mahdi's* followers in another part of the British Empire,[45] that they could not die, are the pioneer forefathers who have long been defamed as syphilis-ridden rapists, murderers and thieves.

The settlers, who had been continually vexed by Te Whiti's followers for years, no longer considered the area safe to develop their land and bring their families and were going to New Plymouth. A young settler by the name of Michael S Deniells, who had recently purchased some land with his brother, had been attacked by a Maori with an axe and when overpowering him had been chased by other Maori. He had returned to New Plymouth because he did not consider it safe to settle his land. Although efforts were made to discredit Daniells' account, he was well-known as a young man of repute, who had no reason to lie, if only because he was trying to get labourers to assist him on his farm.[46]

Te Whiti was given fourteen days by the Government to make his intentions clear and to reach a 'definite understanding'. During this time Government agents visited Te Whiti seeking assurances, yet Te Whiti's only response was to state, 'things must take their course'.

Parihaka's 'Pacifist' Leaders

In 1878 Hiroki, a chief, had murdered a cook. Having been severely wounded by a search party he immediately made his

---

45   At that very time, 1881, Mohammed Ahmed, a cult leader living on an island on the White Nile, had a revelation that he was the Mahdi. This was followed by several decades of fighting the forces of the Mahdi and his successor, which included the famous death of Gen. Gordon at Khartoum.

46   'Native News', *Hawera & Normanby Star*, Volume II, Issue 152, 28 September 1881, p. 3.

way to the safe haven of Parihaka.[47] District Commissioner Parris, in his report to the Under-Secretary of the Native Department, stated that Aperahama Tamaiparea, the principal chief of the Ngarauru tribe, to which Hiroki belonged, went with a party to Parihaka to retrieve Hiroki, but 'the old chief and his party received peremptory orders to leave Parihaka, failing which their lives were threatened'. Tamaiparea and his party withdrew. Parris commented that, 'Criminals of different grades have from time to time taken shelter at Parihaka, and native offenders generally regarded the place as a refuge of safety'.[48] Yet from even before the Bryce raid up to the present, it has been maintained that the 'unease' of the Taranaki settlers in regard to the 'peace maker' Te Whiti, and his followers, was baseless, and even farcical.

Hiroki remained an eminent figure at Parihaka. The attitude of Te Whiti was that Hiroki was a 'refugee' 'under his protection' and he told the Government he would not turn Hiroki over to the Constabulary.[49] When Native Minister Sheehan went to Parihaka to ask for Hiroki to be handed over for trial, Te Whiti continuously interrupted Sheehan, called him a 'thief', harangued Sheehan for half an hour, and said that the Supreme Court should go to Parihaka, and not Hiroki to the court as Hiroki was under his 'protection'.[50] This was megalomania worthy of an African tribal potentate of the Idi Amin or Robert Mugabe variety.

It was not until the occupation of Parihaka by Bryce in November 1881 that Hiroki could finally be brought to trial for murder, for which he was duly hanged. The court heard of how Hiroki would parade about Parihaka with his guns.[51]

Te Whetu, the Parihaka luminary and 'sly grog' seller, was a

---

47   'The Moumaki Murder. Hiroki at Parihaka', *Evening Post*, Volume XVI, Issue 252, 23 October 1878, p. 2.

48   R Parris, Memorandum to the Undersecretary of the Native Department, No. 11, Appendices to the Journal of the House of Representatives, op. cit., G. 1, 1882.

49   'Taranaki Opinion', *Wanganui Herald*, Volume XII, Issue 9455, 25 June 1879, p. 2.

50   'Hiroki's Surrender Refused', *Colonist*, Volume XXII, Issue 2529, 29 March 1879, p. 3.

51   'Trial of Hiroki', *Otago Witness*, Issue 1568, 26 November 1881, p. 11.

notably 'dubious character', and his arrests were accompanied by violence. At the time of Te Whetu's 1880 arrest, the press commented that he is,

> ...a very turbulent and dangerous individual, who is understood to have been guilty of many deeds of violence, and to have openly boasted of them. He was implicated in the murder of Brady at Taranaki some years ago. He is, in fact, a second Te Whiti in influence over a section of the natives, and his capture is one of the best possible things that could have been affected by the Government, as it removes a dangerous firebrand from the district.[52]

Of Titokowaru, James Belich suggests that he entered into an alliance with Te Whiti as early as the 1870s, while Titokowaru was still engaged in armed conflict.[53] Titokowaru's Hau Hau war-cult included cannibalism as a religious sacrament,[54] and the invariable slaying of the wounded.[55] However, the Waitangi Tribunal's resource kit for school students states:

> Titokowaru of Ngati Ruanui was a great leader of the Taranaki people. He tried for many years to keep peace between Taranaki *hapu* and the Government, but the Government kept confiscating more and more Taranaki land. As a last resort, Titokowaru travelled with his people through the war area and cleared it of all soldiers and settlers... [56]

Titokowaru's strategy was to cut off and murder isolated settlers and soldiers, and ambush troops who were sent to restore order.[57]

52 'The Native Difficulty. Arrest of Te Whetu and Others,' *Evening Post*, Volume XX, Issue 167, 20 July 1880, p. 2.
53 J Belich, *The New Zealand Wars* (Auckland: Penguin Books, 1998), p. 272.
54 *Ibid.*, p. 274.
55 *Ibid.*
56 Waitangi Tribunal, 'The Treaty of Waitangi Past and Present, Case Study: Taranaki The End of the Battle', http://www.waitangi-tribunal.govt.nz/resources/school_info/ resourcekitsforschools/whathappenedafterthetreatywassigned.asp
57 W T Parham, *Von Tempsky: Adventurer* (London: Hodder and Stoughton, 1969), p. 194.

VII - 'Passive but Bounceable'

The laudatory remarks on Titokowaru are typical of the tax-funded Government perversion of history that is being used to instil anti-Pakeha sentiment among Maori children and shame among Pakeha children. A contemporary report on the apostle of cannibalism, states in 1869:

> By private letter from Manawapu we receive the following confirmation of the reports, which have been in circulation, telling of cannibalism by Titokowaru in its most revolting form. Blake, who commands the Carlyle Rifles, reports as follows:— A trooper named Smith was killed some months ago in a skirmish at Manutahi, where his remains were buried. It was reported by the mailman that the Hauhaus had exhumed the body, cut off one leg, and eaten it. His supposed grave was pointed out, and Lieutenant Blake, in order to ascertain if the reports were correct, dug up the ground, and sure enough the skeleton was found minus one leg, which had been hacked off by a tomahawk close to the body, and, strange to say, a portion of the thigh bone was found, charred at one end, as though the flesh had been roasted. The bone corresponded with that left on the body, as having the same sort of notches.[58]

Another prominent follower of Te Whiti, Te Mahuki, who was accompanied by a select guard of 'angels' (sic) armed with knives, had tied up two surveyors in the King Country in 1883 and several days later went into Alexandra with the intention of burning it down. That year, after release from jail, he went to Parihaka and was recognised as a prophet by Te Whiti, before proceeding to the Waikato.[59] He had been sentenced to seven years imprisonment for torching Maori houses at Te Kuiti in 1897, ending his days in a lunatic asylum in 1899.

---

58 'Cannibalism by the HauHaus', Daily Southern Cross, Volume XXV, Issue 3762, 9 September 1869, p. 5.
59 'A Maori Fanatic Arrested', *Otago Witness*, Volume 14, Issue 2276, 14 October 1897, p. 53.

There was evident sympathy in Parihaka for murderous acts against the Pakeha, indicated by the collection of donations for a lawyer to defend the murderer of a settler named Stephen Maloney in 1890,[60] who had been killed by a young Maori, Mahi Kai, in the Recreation Grounds.[61] Despite the horrendous nature of the murder - Maloney having been savagely beaten to death for the sake of some boots and clothing - Mahi Kai's death sentence was commuted to life imprisonment.[62] What would have been the result had Mahi Kai murdered a Maori and been judged under Maori law? The outcome would have been *utu* for generations. Yet the common myth today is that Pakeha law did great injustices to the Maori, and the same claim is still being made in regard to the New Zealand justice system.

---

60 'The New Plymouth Murder', North Otago Times, Volume XXXIV, Issue 7023, 21 April 1890, p. 3.

61 'Murder in Recreation Grounds', *Taranaki Herald*, Volume XXXIX, Issue 8906, 14 October 1890, p. 2.

62 'Commutation of New Plymouth Murderer's Sentence', *Bay Of Plenty Times*, Volume XVIII, Issue 2568, 17 December 1890, p. 2.

VIII - Behold a White Horse[1]

The Occupation of Parihaka

The occupation of Parihaka after years of Government vacillation was the achievement of Native Minister John Bryce, who has been maligned ever since. The interim report of the West Coast Commission in 1880 recommended that the Government should do *nothing* about Te Whiti and his campaign of destruction and threats against the settlers, and that he would gradually fade away, stating: 'We believe that if he [Te Whiti] were sure that he would be let alone at Parihaka, he would let us alone on the [Waimate] Plains'.[2] The final Commission report recommended that Maori retain or be given 263,000 acres, with Pakeha having options on 130,000 acres.[3] It should be kept in mind however, that Te Whiti was not even interested in hearing such recommendations. He and his followers had boycotted the Commission because it had declined to go to Parihaka; a reaction typical of Te Whiti's megalomania. All of the land was destined by God to be Te Whiti's.

It is against this background that the mythic status of the raid on Parihaka has been perpetrated. Virginia Winder,[4] writing for *Puke Ariki*,[5] the Taranaki heritage centre sponsored New Plymouth District Council and central Government, states:

1   Bryce was much ridiculed for having entered Parihaka on a white charger.
2   'The Interim Report', *Wanganui Herald*, Volume XII, Issue 3702, 1 May 1880, p. 2.
3   'The final Report of the Royal Commission', *Hawera & Normanby Star*, Volume I, Issue 36, 14 August 1880, p. 2.
4   A local literary luminary and journalism tutor, who also serves as the researcher for New Plymouth District Council's Puke Ariki. Western Institute of Technology Taranaki, http://www.witt.ac.nz/Content/sub/100001700.aspx
5   'Puke Ariki is an innovative museum, library and information centre that combines learning, knowledge, resources and heritage objects for a visitor experience that is like no other', Puke Ariki, 'About Us', http://www.pukeariki.com/PukeAriki/AboutUs.aspx

On 5 November 1881, the peaceful village was invaded by 1500 volunteers and members of the Armed Constabulary. The soldiers were welcomed by the 2000 people of Parihaka, allowing themselves to be arrested without protest.

Te Whiti and Tohu were the first to be led away. They were imprisoned without trial and then taken on a tour of the South Island to show them all the progress and developments made by the Europeans. Neither was impressed,[6] and Te Whiti continued to ask that his people be given justice, their freedom and the return of their tribal lands.[7]

Despite the impression maintained by postmodernist history, Taranaki Maori were greatly perturbed by Te Whiti's actions. In 1879 a delegation of West Coast Maori leaders visited Te Whiti to dissuade him from pursuing his antagonism toward the settlers, as this would only bring 'misfortune on the tribes'.[8] However, Te Whiti, like all cult leaders with a messiah complex, was not going to be dissuaded from his destiny, having spent years contriving a situation that was designed to assure his martyrdom.

On the day of the occupation, Parihaka was 'jammed' with Te Whiti's followers. A representative of Native Affairs Minister Bryce called on Te Whiti with the proclamation to surrender, but Te Whiti made no reply. Half an hour later the Riot Act was read, and an hour elapsed as per law, before the occupation proceeded.[9] Te Whiti had the option of peaceably turning himself

---

6   However, Te Whiti at least took a liking to European cuisine and dining etiquette, which became features of his lavish feasts on his return to Parihaka.

7   V Winder, 'Pacifist of Parihaka – Te Whiti o Rongomai', Puke Ariki, New Plymouth District Council, http://www.pukeariki.com/Research/TaranakiStories/TaranakiStory/id/334/title/pacifist-of-parihaka-te-whiti-o-rongomai.aspx

8   'The Native Difficulty', *West Coast Times*, Issue 3189, 19 June 1879, p. 2.

9   'Arrival at Parihaka', *Nelson Evening Mail*, Volume XVI, Issue XVI, 5 November 1881, p. 2.

and others, including the murderer Hiroki, and the cannibal apostle Titokawaru, over without the need for occupation. In addition, the much-maligned Bryce offered Te Whiti a last minute chance to 'accept the Queen's sovereignty', but he was met with argument.[10]

The alleged conduct of the troops in Parihaka, who are portrayed as rapists, vandals and thieves, seems unlikely. Given that the Native Minister, Bryce, was under criticism from sections of the press and that there had been widespread misgivings about taking action against Te Whiti, the allegations against the Constabulary and Volunteers are more likely to be the product of 19th Century politicking and of anti-Pakeha sentiments. The Constabulary and Volunteers were under close scrutiny, with the presence of several reporters who made much of the burning of *whare* belonging to Maori who had settled there mainly from Wanganui. A flock of spectators stood atop a hill overlooking Parihaka. The historian and folklorist, James Cowan, close to the Maori, who had a pro-Parihaka bias, nonetheless remarked of the Armed Constabulary that they were 'officered by a splendid set of frontier soldiers', and that they had much fighting experience.[11]

Even Dick Scott, author of *The Parihaka Story (1954) and Ask that Mountain* (1975), later concluded that 'Parihaka reports go too far'. Winder writes on the *Puke Ariki* website that Scott 'believes people are now exaggerating the story of Parihaka... It's too one-sided now', he says. 'A huge amount of stuff has been done about Parihaka that's made it much worse than it really was'.

Now he has begun to see grossly inaccurate reports of the powerful story. He has even read where the name of the Waitotoroa River (The River of Long Blood) has been attributed to the day of plunder.

10   K Sinclair, p. 124; citing: 'Report of Meeting at Parihaka', 8. October 1881, 'William Rolleston Papers'.

11   J Cowan, (1922), *The New Zealand Wars and the Pioneering Period* (Wellington: Government Printer, 1983), Vol. 2, p. 494.

'That was a name given at a time of tribal war', Dick says. And while news reports have described Parihaka as New Zealand's equivalent to the holocaust, Dick wants to make it clear: 'No one was killed during (Native Minister John) Bryce's occupation'.

Another discrepancy relates to the dog urinating on the wheel of a cannon pointed at the village. 'I have seen it written that the dog pissed on the gun powder and stopped it firing. It's gone silly the other way'.

Dick also aims criticism at reports from Parihaka saying those taken as prisoners were used to build half the roads in the South Island and that hundreds died.[12]

Allegations of rape by Government forces at Parihaka were made by a witness, who testified at a commission of enquiry 'more than forty years later', claiming that soldiers 'assaulted the womenfolk' and some were made pregnant. Related to this is the often-stated story of the spread of syphilis.[13] Dick Scott wrote that he had confirmed the accounts of an outbreak of syphilis, having been told by Dr Edward Pohau Ellison[14] that, 'He had treated a number of people who had syphilis - the troops had infected the people'.[15] The claim that troops had raped the women and infected them with syphilis seems to be speculation, and could be accounted for by the propensity since the earliest days of Pakeha settlement, of chiefs giving their *wahine* over to prostitution, a plausible explanation in the case of Parihaka,

12 V Winder, 'Scott: Parihaka Reports go too far', Puke Ariki, 20 October, 2003. New Plymouth District Council, http://www.pukeariki.com/Research/TaranakiStories/TaranakiStory/id/92/title/scott-parihaka-reports-go-too-far.aspx

13 A present-day account from the organisers of the Parihaka International Peace Festival, states: 'Women and girls were raped leading to an outbreak of syphilis in the community'. http://www.parihaka.com/About.aspx

14 Ellison, who was raised in Taranaki, replaced Dr Peter Buck as director of the Division of Maori Hygiene in the Department of Health in 1927.

15 V Winder, 'Dick Scott outlines own Parihaka Journey', Puke Ariki, http://www.pukeariki.com/Research/TaranakiStories/TaranakiStory/id/90/title/dick-scott-outlines-own-parihaka-journey.aspx

given its history as a centre of contagion, and of Te Whiti's interest in profiting from his followers by seemingly every possible means. Information available to the Government on the incidence of venereal disease among the Maori prior to 1939 was 'at best, anecdotal'.[16]

The introduction of prostitution is one of many evils frequently ascribed to the coming of the Pakeha colonists. However *The Prow*, in describing pre-colonial slavery among the Maori, states:

> As in many other cultures, slavery was a key element of Maori society. *Mokai*[17] were usually spoils of war, condemned to lives of drudgery, danger, heavy physical work and obedience to their masters or mistresses' whims; they were expected to fight under supervision, could be used to negotiate with enemies, or as food if supplies were short. Female slaves might be prostitutes, or become secondary wives to their conquerors. Marriages between victorious chiefs and highborn women of defeated tribes strengthened the invaders *take* to the land.[18]

Whatever one calls it, the selling of women into servitude, including sexual servitude, was a feature of Maori society both before and after the arrival of the Pakeha. When single white males began coming to New Zealand in increasing numbers, Maori prostitution became lucrative business, but was not something that had been introduced. The parading of women in their best clothing before Pakeha guests at Parihaka, for which the women had to pay Te Whiti, and which drew the ire of Tohu, is yet to be explained.

---

16 A Kampf, *'This Racial Menace'?: Public Health, Venereal Disease and Maori in New Zealand, 1930-1947'*, US National Library of Medicine, Maryland, Medical History, 51(4): 435–452, 1 October 1; 2007.

17 Slaves.

18 'Slavery in Pre-Colonial Times', TheProw.org, described as: 'The Prow is a collaboration between the Nelson City, Tasman and Marlborough District Libraries, Nelson Marlborough Institute of Technology and The Nelson Provincial Museum'. http://www.theprow.org.nz/

Another allegation is that hundreds of pigs, cattle and horses were killed or taken away.[19] A contemporary report states,

> Some Volunteers killed two Maori pigs, but the Natives have taken no notice of it…. Strict orders have been issued to the Constabulary and Volunteers not to interfere with Maori property of any kind at Parihaka.[20]

The proceedings were observed by several members of the press, one writing: '…Not an action escaped observation. Not an order given was unheard or unrecorded'.[21] There was also a body of spectators who had gathered atop the hill in front of Parihaka.[22] Despite the outrage of some press reporters at the arrest of Te Whiti and Tohu and of the destruction of *whare* belonging to those from outside communities, there is no mention in the reports of the later allegations of rape, looting and the slaughter of livestock.

The first Commission of Enquiry on Parihaka (1882) and contemporary newspaper accounts, refer to the searching of households as 'pillaging'[23] and hence the fiction has been maintained of mass looting, whereas the property was presented to Bryce for inspection, including a stockpile of weapons.[24]

As has been indicated throughout this book, despite what one might assume, the colonial press and other influential sections of European colonial society, were by no means universally antagonistic towards Te Whiti. It was also by no means universally accepted that Bryce had undertaken the right course,

19   Te Miringa Hohaia, Gregory O'Brien, Lara Strongman, Parihaka: The Art of Passive Resistance (Wellington: City Gallery, 2001), 'Te Pahuatangha O Parihaka', Hazel Riseborough. p. 37.
20   'Latest Intelligence', *Taranaki Herald*, op. cit.
21   R W Rusden, p. 111.
22   'Latest Intelligence', *Taranaki Herald*, Volume XXIX, Issue 3884, 7 November 1881, p. 2.
23   R W Rusden, p. 113.
24   'Successful seizure', *Manawatu Times*, Volume V, Issue 173, 12 November 1881, Page 3.

and he was not immune from criticism by the press. In fact, Bryce was condemned by some of the press for his breaking of the Parihaka stronghold, and it was even compared as a shameful act to the persecution of the Huguenots of France in a poem published in the *Observer*.[25] Given that there were reporters who had secreted themselves in Parihaka[26] and other civilians there, including Government officials, it seems likely that had there been the mass of rapes, looting and other depredations that are now central to the Parihaka Myth, there would have been more than the reporting of the killing of several pigs.[27]

Weapons and Murderers

While one of the most prominent features of the Parihaka Myth is the passivity and even the amiability of the Maori towards the occupying troops, Native Minister Bryce had been informed by a Maori who had just come from Parihaka, that there would not be armed resistance because 'there were too many soldiers now'.[28] The implication was that this was the only option because of being out-gunned. There were weapons stocked at Parihaka, and a significant proportion of those with violent temperaments, including honoured murderers such as Hiroki, and Titokowaru with his cannibal band. With the occupation of Parihaka pending, information had been received that those at Parihaka were discussing war and that they had plenty of arms and ammunition.[29] What transpired when Bryce's forces occupied Parihaka was the seizure of 250 weapons, including breechloaders, Enfields and revolvers, and a variety of ammunition.[30] The *Hawera Star* reported:

25   'Hon. Mr Bryce', *Observer*, Volume 3, Issue 74, 11 February 1882, p. 339.
26   'Latest Intelligence', *Taranaki Herald*, op. cit.
27   The actual slaughter of the large herd of pigs at Parihaka occurred in 1887 when some trespassed onto the burial ground, and disturbed bodies. Since it could not be ascertained which specific pigs were involved in the act, all the pigs were 'brained' by order of Te Whiti. 'The Porcine Slaughter at Parihaka', *Taranaki Herald*, Volume XXXVI, Issue 7960, 2 September 1887, p. 2.
28   'The Native Crisis', *Evening Post*, Volume XXII, Issue 108, 4 November 1881, p. 2.
29   'Security for Peace Gone', *Star*, Issue 4226, 7 November 1881, p. 3.
30   'Latest Native Intelligence', *Tuapeka Times*, Volume XIV, Issue 787, 9 November 1881,

Guns and ammunition of all kinds were found in the *whares*, and brought out and piled close to where the Ministers were seated. The number of rifles discovered perfectly bears out the report of your correspondent two years back, as many as 10 being found in one *whare*.[31]

The attitude of Titokowaru was less than pacifistic, telling Captain Northcroft, 'Your day will come soon; have you forgotten Motumoa and Te Ngutu o te Manu?'[32] Te Mgatu o te Manu was Titokowaru's *pa*, which had been attacked by Government forces in 1868 in retaliation for a Ruanui attack on a Government outpost. It was a major defeat for the Government, during which the famous Maj. Gustavus Von Temsky was killed.[33] What the apostle of cannibalism was threatening was that there would be *utu* for the attack on Parihaka. Meeting the night prior to the Government occupation, Titokowaru's men had been eager to offer armed resistance but the chief forbade this because of the superior forces of the Government.[34]

It was these men from Ngati Ruanui who had in former days feasted on their victims, killed the wounded, and to whom Te Whiti had referred as the tribe of Benjamin, citing *Genesis* in regard to ravening wolves and despoilers. Was Bryce expected to enter Parihaka without preparing for the exigency of a violent conflict from several thousand Maori drawn from far and wide, who had for years been inculcated with a fanatical belief that Te Whiti was a godlike being who could raise them from the dead? Yet, despite the manner by which colonial New Zealand is today portrayed, press commentary shows that not only was there a widespread desire to see the settlement of Maori land grievances, which all New Zealanders should today realise has always been a hopeless tangle, but that Bryce was subjected to

---

p. 3.

31   'Resistance Not for the Want of Arms', Star, Issue 4227, 8 Nov 1881, p. 3.
32   'Latest from the Front' *Thames Star*, Volume XII, Issue 4024, 21 Nov 1881 p 2.
33   'Attack on Te Ngutu o te Manu', http://www.teara.govt.nz/en/ngati-ruanui/3/3
34   'A Vindication', *Wanganui Herald*, Volume XXXVII, Issue 10871, 11 Feb 1903, p. 4.

much ridicule after the Parihaka venture by those who could afford to jest at a safe distance. Parodied, for example in a poem carried in *The Thames Star*, the editor delighted in the ridicule of Bryce and his men:

> Te Whiti and Tohu were taking a rest
> Their wives and their people around 'em
> We brought the old warriors out of their nest
> Then collar'd Hiroki, and bound him.
>
> Few and short were the words they said
> They looked not in anger but sorrow
> They steadfastly gazed on us shaking each head,
> As they bitterly thought of the morrow....
>
> ...slowly but surely our Gen'ral go down
> From his charger all white, framed in story;
> And telegrams flashed to each city and town
> The news of Jack Bryce and his glory.[35]

The primary aim of Bryce was to disperse the inhabitants of Parihaka, who had come from far and wide, back to their own communities. He telegrammed the Government that he had succeeded better than expected in separating 600 women and 400 children for their return by steamer to Wanganui.[36] Given that 1000 of those at Parihaka were women and children from Wanganui, the question arises as to the nature of the demographics of Parihaka and the use of women and children by Te Whiti. They had long been sent on missions of vandalism against settlers, and were used as front line obstructions during the Parihaka occupation, in a cynical move that has become quite typical of protestors today.

The treatment accorded to Tohu and Te Whiti during their

---

35 Frank Fudge, 'The Battle of Parihaka', *Thames Star*, Volume XII, Issue 4058, 31 Dec 1881, p. 2.

36 'Affairs at Parihaka', *Manawatu Times*, Volume V, Issue 173, 16 November 1881, p. 2.

detention was extremely accommodating. Riseborough states that they were given tweed suits, toured about the country, and were placed under house detention, her main point in describing the humane treatment being that the two prophets could not be 'bought',[37] rather than commending the authorities on their forbearance. Historian Keith Sinclair writes that Te Whiti and Tohu spent over a year travelling around the South Island, 'being treated as gentlemen and not as convicts'.[38] Despite refusing to negotiate, they were permitted to return to Parihaka in 1883, to resume their strategy of vandalism and theft. The bloodthirsty old war chief Titokowaru was not prosecuted.[39]

Although it is stated that the Government, having dressed Te Whiti and Tohu in tweed suits and shown them the benefits of European civilisation, did not succeed in winning them over to Pakeha ways, this does not seem to be entirely accurate. Te Whiti stated that he was 'very hospitably entertained' while in detention. There was a widespread feeling among Maori that Te Whiti had become 'all the same as the Pakeha'.[40]

Productive Interregnum

With the arrest of Te Whiti and Tohu, the occupants of Parihaka were said to have returned to an 'idle and indolent' state and were awaiting Te Whiti's 'coming in the clouds from the South Island'.[41] Naturally, the state of Te Whiti's followers with the departure of their leaders and the dispersal of outsiders back to their own communities, is blamed on the Bryce raid rather than on the demands Te Whiti had made on his followers.[42]

---

37   H Riseborough,., p. 40.
38   K Sinclair, p. 124.
39   *Ibid.*, p. 124.
40   'Affairs at Parihaka' *Manawatu Standard*, Volume 3, Issue 39, 21 Mar 1883, p. 2.
41   'The Parihaka Natives', *West Coast Times*, Issue 4123, July 3 1882, p. 2.
42   As one would expect, the Waitangi Tribunal places all responsibility for the plight of Te Whiti's followers on Bryce, and upholds Te Whiti and Tohu as great prophets and leaders, and Parihaka as part of a 'living tradition'. The Taranaki Report: Kaupapa Tuatahi, 8.17, 'The Invasion'.

However, the present-day 'history' perpetrated by the Waitangi Tribunal and others not withstanding, with the detaining of Tohu and Te Whiti, and the prohibition of the monthly gatherings at Parihaka to pay tribute to Te Whiti, orderly cultivation of lands was soon resumed in the District. In October 1882 Bryce visited Parihaka. Reports state that potato seeds were being delivered to other parts of the District on an almost daily basis. Tumoake, the chief presiding over Parihaka in the absence of Tohu and Te Whiti, commented on the manner by which 'strangers' had already caused enough trouble at Parihaka, and welcomed the Government's prevention of outside migrations.[43]

With Te Whiti and Tohu gone Parihaka and other communities in the District, soon entered a productive state not seen for years, a press report stating:

> ...The West Coast Maoris ... have done a good deal of substantial fencing by means of ditch and bank... Several large canoes for fishing have been constructed. In all their fencing and cultivations the Maoris have confined themselves to the lands assigned them and kept within the boundaries fixed... and on all hands the Native Minister is said to have received assurances that the temper of the West Coast natives has very much changed for the better.[44]

Regression

With the return of Te Whiti and Tohu matters soon regressed. In 1885 the rents from leased farms were refused and more money was demanded, otherwise the land would be taken back from the Europeans. The press was again reporting in familiar manner:

> The Natives show a determined opposition to settlers, trying

---

43 'Mr Bryce's Visit to Parihaka', *Wanganui Chronicle*, Volume XXIV, Issue 9662, 3 October 1882, p. 2.
44 'Native affairs at Parihaka', *Taranaki Herald*, Volume XXX, Issue 4153, 3 October 1882, p. 2.

to annoy them in every possible way. When Native cattle trespass on the cultivated lands of Europeans, the Natives, instead of taking the cattle out through slip bars, deliberately demolish the fences, or cut down the ditch and bank, as the case may be, and take their cattle away. This causes heavy loss to settlers, who see no way of obtaining redress.[45]

The situation for the settlers seemed worse than ever. That year a rival to the divine status of Te Whiti was being claimed by Reri, who stated that he had been appointed by the Government to rule over Maori, and that he had the divine power to kill wicked Maori and Pakeha. While Te Whiti could do nothing about Tohu who had a large rival following, he was able to have Reri committed to an asylum.[46] Perhaps Te Whiti did not see the irony.

The attitude of the Government towards Te Whiti and Parihaka remained deferential. In 1895 Premier Seddon arrived in Patea on his way to Parihaka to meet with Te Whiti. A delegation of Maori led by Tutangi met the Premier, and urged him not to make the visit, as it gave the impression of subordination and 'the premier was a bigger man than Te Whiti and Tohu, and should not go to them'. 'All the speakers took this line, Ngapaki remarking that the natives here were Queen's Maoris, and did not want to have anything to do with Te Whiti'.[47] Ngapaki said that he thought the Premier did not understand the significance that would be attached to his coming to Te Whiti. Tutangi said that Te Whiti and Tohu 'had caused a great deal of trouble'.[48]

Deaths of Te Whiti and Tohu

Tohu and Te Whiti both died in 1907. By that time the two had become rivals with their separate followings. Tohu had a far

45   'The Parihaka Natives', Star, Issue 5311, 15 May 1885, p. 4.
46   'Two of a Trade', West Coast Times, Issue 4824, 23 January 1885, p. 2.
47   'The Premier and the Natives', Nelson Evening Mail, Volume XXIX, Issue 114, 16 May 1895, p. 3.
48   'The Premier at Taranaki. Addresses of Maori Chiefs', Evening Post, Volume XLIX, Issue 115, 16 May 1895, p. 2.

larger following than Te Whiti. A gathering to determine the future of the Tohu faction met after their prophet's death. One of Tohu's colleagues, Te Kahupohoro, paid tribute to Tohu's 'supernatural powers', including his ability to prophesy the failure of a potato crop, the death of a prime minister, and the admonition not to trust Pakeha. The warrior Tauke, on the other hand, who had believed in Tohu, asked how a prophet could die? He could no longer believe in Tohu, but neither would he follow Te Whiti. Three chiefs urged those present not to follow Te Whiti, 'who took their money and only gave them prophecies of doubtful merit in return'.[49]

A delegation of the Young Maori Party stated that now Tohu was dead it was an opportunity to be rid of the influence of Parihaka altogether. Te Whiti, they stated, was a fraud who could do no good for Maori. They urged the Maori to work their land, rather than throwing money away on Te Whiti.[50]

Te Whiti died soon afterwards. A newspaper correspondent, whose tone was reverential, remarked that around 1200 Maori were present and about an equal number of Pakeha. He was surprised at the relatively low Maori attendance, and considered it a measure that Te Whiti's *mana* had already died. [51] Te Whiti's followers wanted a grand burial, while those of Tohu said that Te Whiti, 'buried his followers like a dog; why not bury him like a dog?' The European dignitaries seemed to have expressed far greater admiration than some of the Maori. Homi, the son-in-law of the late Tohu, pacing and pointing his stick, vehemently declared to the gathering,

It serves you right, you tribes, to have believed these two men (Tohu and Te Whiti)... Talk about words. Wind! What

---

49   'The Parihaka Influence. Young Maoris Efforts to Break it. Tohuites Decline to Join Te
      Whiti. Parihaka Pilgrimages Probably Past', *Wanganui Herald*, Volume XXXXI, Issue
      12106, February 28 1907, p. 3.
50   'The Parihaka Influence', *Wanganui Herald*, op. cit.
51   'The Parihaka Tangi. The Burial of Te Whiti', *Hawera & Normanby Star*, Volume LIII,
      Issue 9480, November 23 1907, p. 5.

is the use of their predictions; they have all come wrong. You have been duped! ... These men were past masters in word-painting; that is all! You have been deceived. You should have awakened to that fact. [52]

---

52   'The Parihaka Tangi', *Hawera & Normanby Star, Ibid.*

IX - Aftermath: John Bryce and Billy Te Whiti

In 1884 Native Minister John Bryce proceeded with a libel action against historian G W Rusden, who had written a precursor of the present-day Parihaka and anti-Pakeha literature. Rusden claimed that when Bryce was a Lieutenant with the Kai Iwi Cavalry he had rushed down on Maori women and children, 'cutting them down gleefully and with ease'.[1] Rusden attempted in his defence to prove that 'Bryce was of a naturally cruel and headstrong disposition"[2] by referring to the later action at Parihaka. The allegations were fully aired in a British Court, where it was disclosed that Rusden had been misinformed about Bryce by Bishop Hadfield of Wellington, and by the former Governor, Sir Arthur Gordon. This alone indicates what opposition Bryce had encountered among colonial luminaries.

The former Native Affairs Minister, despite having been slandered by certain sections of the press, Government and Church, was by then widely called 'Honest John Bryce'. Rusden, through the machinations of Bishop Hadfield and Sir Arthur Gordon, had been induced to portray Bryce as 'cruel, cowardly and heartless', in his *History of New Zealand*. A press report of the time referring to Parihaka states that the evidence at the British Court had removed 'a great stain from the colony whose reputation must have lately suffered [had it] allowed to remain unrefuted'. Under cross-examination, 'fully conscious of his absolute innocence in this matter', Bryce answered 'promptly and satisfactorily'. Efforts were made at Court to try and justify Rusden's portrayal of Bryce by claiming that the Minister undertook a 'cruel and

---

1   'Obituary. Mr G W Rusden', *Evening Post*, Volume LXVI, Issue 152, 24 December 1903, p. 5.

2   *West Coast Times* , Issue 6207, 5 May 1886, p. 2.

wicked course' at Parihaka.[3] Interestingly, despite the attempts to blacken Bryce's name and Rusden's insistence that the Parihaka incident was 'cruel', no mention was made of women being raped, or any other such brutalities. The report comments that New Zealanders still remembered how there had been no cruelty undertaken in Parihaka against the Maori in Bryce's detention of Tohu and Te Whiti.[4] Had atrocities taken place under Bryce's command at Parihaka, sections of the press, Hadfield, Gordon, et al would certainly have capitalised on this.

In 1886, according to the *Taranaki Daily News*, 'Te Whiti's daughter... was in court ... repenting [her] misuse of Parihaka funds sent by New Zealand supporters and foreigners, mainly in Parihaka Bank', an event 'generously glossed over' by Dick Scott, states Jean Jackson.[5]

According to an absurdly sycophantic article on Te Whiti in *The Journal of the Polynesian Society*, where all the old clichés about The Prophet's genius are trotted out, the funds that had been accrued, supposedly to be used when God had restored Maori over New Zealand, were embezzled after Te Whiti's death in 1907.[6] The use of funds and other donated largesse for personal aggrandisement was a feature of the Te Whiti cult, and in keeping with the mentality of Third World potentates past and present.

In 1918 Te Whiti's son Billy was involved in a violent fracas with police at Rahotu. When constable O'Neill attempted to arrest Billy Te Whiti a war cry came up which was responded to by seventy Maori. The Constable called for help and about a half dozen Pakeha came forth. The affray ensued for about an hour,

3   'Bryce vs. Rusden', *Evening Post*, Volume XXXI, Issue 101, 1 May 1886, p.1.
4   'Bryce vs. Rusden', *Nelson Evening Mail*, Volume XX, Issue 92, 19 April 1886, p. 2.
      In 1887 in an out-of-court settlement, Bryce waived £1300 of the £5000 that had been awarded to him against Rusden. 'Bryce vs. Rusden', Ashburton Guardian, Volume V, Issue 1588, 18 June 1887, p. 2.
5   Jean Jackson, op. cit.
6   Bernard Gadd, p. 454, citing, McMaster, p. 141.

until Billy Te Whiti escaped. The Constable was badly bruised, and one Pakeha had his finger almost bitten off.[7] Te Whiti's son was putting his father's metaphors into practice.

---

7   'Serious Disturbance', Colonist, Volume LX, Issue 146734, 1 April 1918, p. 6.

Conclusion

In 1903 the question of the propriety of the Parihaka invasion was revisited in a debate in the press relating to the publication of a book in London by Christchurch author and jurist O T J Alpers, entitled *New Zealand in the Nineteenth Century*. Parihaka, as shown, has always had its Pakeha apologists. When the *Christchurch Press* critiqued the book, Alpers wrote a lengthy response lauding Te Whiti as a great prophet and a man of peace, and condemning the occupation by Government forces as a travesty against innocent women and children. *The Press* provided its own spirited reply to Alpers, stating that regardless of the question as to whether Te Whiti intended violence, the real issue was one of whether he constituted a menace to order and good government. In 1879 Te Whiti had started ploughing up settlers' properties 'in a most thorough way. The manner was so aggressive that the residents in the district who had been through one Maori war, had no doubt that this was merely the prelude to another'. Governor Sir Hercules Robinson and Premier Sir George Grey visited the district and considered the situation so dire as to put all settlers under arms.[1]

In 1908, at the unveiling of a memorial to Te Whiti very few Maori were in attendance. About three hundred Maori from outside Parihaka had come to pay homage. Taare Waitara, Te Whiti's son-in-law, expressed disappointment at the small attendance, but compared the memorial scroll in importance to the tablets of Moses.[2] It seems that the spell of Te Whiti had been broken, and would lie dormant until being resurrected in more

---

1   'A Page of Taranaki History. The Parihaka Incident Reviewed. Newspaper Controversy in Christchurch', *Taranaki Herald*, Volume L, Issue 12176, 27 January 1903, p. 6.
2   'In Memory of Te Whiti', *Taranaki Herald*, Volume LIV, Issue 13729, 19 August 1908, p. 2.

recent years as an integral part of the anti-Pakeha agenda.

In 1914, the deaths of both Tohu and Te Whiti having taken place seven years previously, the Governor and the Native Minister Hon. W H Herries, were invited to Parihaka, with Herries reporting that he was pleased that the antagonism against Pakeha that had been a feature of the old regime had now gone. Herries stated, 'the people showed a very good feeling towards his Excellency and towards the Government':

> They indicated in their speeches that they were satisfied with the Native legislation passed during the last two sessions. In my capacity as Native Minister, I remained behind to hear complaints, but very few were brought forward. The old barrier between the Te Whitis and Tohuites in Parihaka has broken-down. There is just a little jealousy between the Native sections, but none between them, and the pakeha. The Parihaka Natives are quite prepared to take their place as citizens of the Dominion, instead of holding aloof as they have done for so many years.[3]

With the deaths of the cult leaders the unfolding of a new era seemed imminent, just as it had for a year when Te Whiti and Tohu had been detained. Some of the great names in Maoridom formed the Young Maori Party, and had become influential in Government, in medicine, and scholarship, and were achieving a renaissance among Maori. It has only been in recent decades that the process has been reversed, again. New interpretations are being given to the 'Treaty of Waitangi' as a 'living document' and an apparently endless process of 'full and final settlements' under the Treaty, for grievances that have been 'fully and finally settled' many times over, have wreaked havoc on Maori-Pakeha relations, under the grey blanket of a contrived anti-Pakeha sentiment. The Parihaka Myth is a component of this.

---

3   'The Te Whiti Movement. Last Vestiges of Antagonism', Colonist, Volume LVI, Issue 13423, 21 March 1914, p. 7.

Conclusion

After criticism of the former Native Minister, William Rolleston, then on his deathbed, had been made by Alpers in 1903, Bryce broke his silence about Parihaka and responded to *The Press* with a number of matters that had long been forgotten. Bryce reminded readers that Rolleston had continually sought a settlement of grievances with Te Whiti, but had been rebuffed and the messiah had not allowed his followers to hear anything of the terms. Bryce suggested that Te Whiti's intransigence was based on his belief in being God, having established the burial ground close to the *marae* so that when he raised the dead, 'they would have less trouble in joining the living'. Bryce wrote:

His numerous visitors, month after month after many months, brought clothes with them for the dead who were to be quickened into life. Why should they listen to the wretched Pakeha? When Titokowaru asked him on a noted occasion who was behind him to enable him to do the things he spoke of, Te Whiti replied, in a voice which rang over the countryside: 'There is no one behind me; I am the Father; I am the Son, I am the Holy Ghost; there is no one behind me'; and Titokowaru sat down with a muttered apology. Visits of Ministers, indeed! - Reserves, Supreme Court! Pooh! Why do white people talk folly? It was only when threatened by an overwhelming force that Te Whiti's natural timidity overcame his superstition. That Te Whiti's ideas were wider than the West Coast of this island, or even the whole of New Zealand, I may endeavour to show on a future occasion, but that is not the point just now. The point is that Rolleston did everything that mortal man could do to ensure by negotiation a settlement without force, and at last had to give up the attempt in despair. Prior to the request that I should resume office, Rolleston had made all suitable arrangements to secure, by a display of force, a peaceful termination of a disagreeable and dangerous drama.[4]

---

4   'A Vindication', *Wanganui Herald*, Volume XXXVII, Issue 10871, 11 February 1903,

The Parihaka Cult

Bryce related that although the Constabulary and Volunteers were ill prepared for a surprise attack, he was by no means certain that they would not be greeted with armed resistance. This uncertainty was understandable as, despite the pretensions about being the prophet of peace, Te Whiti was clearly psychotic, and Bryce obviously knew this. Yet Bryce, whilst known in his time as an honourable gentlemen and having been a brave soldier, has been vilified from his own time to the present. Even in 1922 the historian and folklorist James Cowan compared Bryce unfavourably to Te Whiti, and wrote that 'history has vindicated the grey old man of Parihaka'.[5]

The mythologizing of the evil Bryce and the godly Te Whiti, as one would expect, has increased with time. One of Te Whiti's present-day exponents, Hazel Riseborough refers to Bryce as 'fanatical'[6] and the Parihaka occupation as 'Bryce's day of shame',[7] while Te Whiti and Tohu are ascribed only the most admirable of traits. Yet despite the negative quips against Bryce as Native Minister, historian Keith Sinclair states of him that he was concerned that Maori were selling their land and urged them to lease it instead, legislating as Minister to remove the abuses of direct purchase.[8] In 1880 Bryce introduced a Bill by which a commissioner appointed by the Governor would be empowered to validate contracts between Europeans and Maori when such contracts had been made prior to the force of law, thereby ensuring that the contracts would be honoured. A second Bill was introduced by Bryce by which district Waste Land Boards would act as the trustees of Maori land to ensure that all owners wished to sell or lease, and to oversee the sale at auction in the same way as Crown Lands were sold.[9]

p. 4.
5   J Cowan (1922), The New Zealand Wars and the Pioneering Period (Wellington: Government Printer, 1983), Vol. 2, p. 488.
6   H Riseborough, 'A New Kind of Resistance', Chapter 11, p. 231; K Day (ed.) Contested Ground: The Taranaki Wars (Wellington: Huia Publications, 2010).
7   *Ibid.*, p. 248.
8   K Sinclair, p. 82.
9   'Native Land Legislation', Hawke's Bay Herald, Volume XXI, Issue 5716, 16 June 1880, p. 2.

Conclusion

The apologetics of Mr Alpers dating back to 1903 are now the orthodox version of Parihaka, but the issues raised in the cogent reply by the *Christchurch Press* have long been consigned to the memory hole. What remains is a one-sided mythologizing of Parihaka as yet another part of an anti-Pakeha agenda. The portrayal most favoured today is that of the type featured by Riseborough who refers to Tohu and Te Whiti as 'Parihaka's two remarkable leaders', whose 'peaceful legacy' has been maintained despite all the provocations, denigration and injustice. An annual 'Parihaka International Peace Festival' was inaugurated in March 2006, attended by '8000 friendly, smiling people' with three days of music, art and traditional healing, on the Parihaka *marae*. 'The influence of Te Whiti and Tohu lives on'.[10]

An account of the 2009 festival provides a different picture:

> The peace at Parihaka was mainly drug-induced, leading South Taranaki Maori warden Imelda Mauriri says.

> 'I saw 10-year-olds and 11-year-olds smoking cannabis. I saw parents so stoned they could not find their babies. It was disgusting,' she said. 'Parihaka is supposed to be a religious and spiritual festival. The organisers and participants have got this confused with being stoned.'

> 'I was there for the three days of the festival. They were peaceful because so many were stoned. Cannabis was freely available, and herbal happy pills. I'm very concerned because it's our own Maori people who are condoning this.

> 'I'm worried this is the pattern for the future. I'm worried that young people will be exposed to this drugs culture and think it's normal. It won't stay peaceful when drugs are involved.'[11]

---

10   H Riseborough, p. 252.
11   'Parihaka Crowd "Stoned"', Taranaki Daily News, 12 January 2009.

While Imelda Mauriri thought that Te Whiti would have been horrified by the conduct, his propensity for selling 'sly grog', and possibly as a purveyor of prostitutes to the Pakeha, might suggest that if he were to return messiah-style today he would be inclined towards a 'slice of the action'.

The attitude of the state's Waitangi Tribunal gives official sanction to the mythologising of Parihaka and its use in ongoing anti-Pakeha agendas, its resource kit for schools stating:

The families have not forgotten all the terrible things that happened to their people. Parents told their children what happened, and when those children grew up, they told their children, and so on till the present day'.[12]

The propagation of the Parihaka cult in publishing continues, with new books such as *The Parihaka Album*,[13] and the novel *The Parihaka Woman*.[14] As this is written there has premiered a film, 'Tatarakihi: The Children of Parihaka', the description being:

In 1881 the children of Parihaka greeted the government invaders with white feathers of peace. Tatarakihi tells the story of a 'journey of memory' taken by a group of Parihaka children who travel to the South Island 130 years later. They follow in the footsteps of their male ancestors who were transported south after the Taranaki land confiscations of the 1860s. Wellington War Memorial, Addington Jail and Ripapa Island in Lyttelton Harbour are key stations on the long bus journey to the caves at Andersons Bay in Dunedin where the Parihaka men were imprisoned. The

---

12 Waitangi Tribunal, 'The Treaty of Waitangi Past and Present, Case Study: Taranaki, The Situation Today', http://www.waitangi-tribunal.govt.nz/resources/school_info/resourcekitsforschools/whathappenedafterthetreatywassigned.asp
13 Rachel Buchanan, The Parihaka Album, 2010
14 Witi Ihimaera, The Parihaka Woman, 2011.

prisoners were forced to labour on buildings, roads and embankments. These enduring expressions of Dunedin's 19th-century prosperity were founded on something closely resembling slavery. Ensuring that the experience of the slaves endures as well, the passage of knowledge conveyed in and by Tatarakihi is both sombre and enriching. The film is narrated by the children and combines footage of their hikoi (some of it shot by the children themselves) with vivid archival photography.[15]

'Tatarakihi' was shown as part of the 2012 New Zealand International Film Festival. The main ingredients of postmodernism and postcolonialism are there: The focus is on the greeting of the supposedly 'brutal' colonial troops by children holding white feathers, without consideration given to the cynical exploitation of women and children as part of Te Whiti's psychotic quest for martyrdom. The theme of the film is the metamorphosing of Maori prisoners from penal labourers to 'slaves' (sic) with all the loaded, propagandistic connotations of that word. Hence, it can now be claimed that 'New Zealand had Maori slaves', whereas the only slavery that existed in New Zealand was among the Maori. The existence of slavery in New Zealand therefore becomes a Pakeha rather than a Maori responsibility. However penal labour for road building and other public works was a common feature of sentencing for prisoners regardless of race.

Of these Taranaki prisoners, a judicial report in 1873 states that the prisoners were released under an amnesty, Resident Magistrate, Isaac Newton Watt, describing them as 'exceptional prisoners, who were treated exceptionally'.[16] Moreover, the 74 prisoners had been part of Titokowaru's utterly ruthless cannibal cult, later to become the 'Benjaminite's' of Parihaka under Te Whiti. That prisoners of the viciousness of these were

---

15   'Tatarakihi: The Children of Parihaka'.
16   New Zealand Historical Places Trust, citing: Isaac Newton Watt, 31 March 1873.

amnestied, having been given maximum sentences of seven years, indicates the forbearance, to the point of weakness, of the Colonial Administration.

On 3 November 2011, a delegation of the 'Parihaka Movement' held a commemoration ceremony on the grounds of Parliament. In response Members of Parliament for the Maori Party presented a petition to Parliament calling for a 'Parihaka Day' for 5 November, to replace Guy Fawkes Day, which they dismissed as an irrelevant vestige of British custom. In 2012 it was reported that the push by Taranaki Maori and Maori Party Members of Parliament to have a commemorative day established for Parihaka is gaining momentum. *The Taranaki Daily News* reported:

> Yesterday, Maori Party senior adviser Chris McKenzie told the Taranaki Daily News they were moving in the right direction to make the dream a reality. Mr McKenzie said there were no plans to drop Guy Fawkes entirely but instead offer a day for New Zealanders to celebrate their history and each other.

> It would create balance to Waitangi Day that was often seen as a flashpoint for cultural debate, he said. 'We need a day when we can talk about things that are tough and Waitangi Day provides that opportunity. We also need a day for celebration'. Mr McKenzie said once the bill was drafted it would be dropped into the private members' ballot, and due to their confidence and supply agreement with the Government it would get past the first reading. 'At the very least'. However, they wouldn't sit on their hands waiting for it to be plucked out and could approach the Government to run with it itself. 'We aren't worried whose name is on top of it', he said. 'We expect this to get overwhelming support'.

> Provincial iwi leaders agree and say the proposed national

day was long overdue. Nga Hapu o Ngaruahine Iwi Incorporated chairwoman Daisy Noble said it was time to push Guy Fawkes aside and embrace a day with national significance. 'I think it's a good thing. It was a key event in our history that must be remembered'. She said far from being a day to point the finger it would be about coming together and celebrating the good in the country. Te Atiawa Iwi Authority chairwoman Wikitoria Keenan said it was time to accept what happened and move on. 'I don't think we should be scared of our past. I think we should acknowledge it'.

Maori identity Peter Moeahu cut straight to the point. 'What better cause to celebrate than peace on earth and goodwill to all mankind. If we can't celebrate that as a nation then I think something is wrong'. No-one from Parihaka could be reached for comment yesterday, but the Daily News understands its people are relieved politicians are finally taking the idea seriously.[17]

In keeping with the New Zealand mentality of the past several decades, it is likely there will be a 'Parihaka Day' celebrating another distortion of New Zealand history whilst denigrating the settler heritage. As reported above, Maori interests are confident of this. Such a 'commemorative day', despite the assurances that there will be 'no finger pointing' at the Pakeha, will intrinsically be a day of anti-Pakeha defamation, founded on the postmodernist falsification of history to serve an agenda. The rhetoric already about 'celebrating peace and goodwill to all' indicates the falsified character of any such celebration. A Parihaka commemorative day is analogous to the US commemoration of a Jonestown Day to celebrate Reverend Jim Jones and his Guyana colony as the heralds of 'peace and goodwill to all', which is how they were indeed once regarded by liberal political celebrities.

---

17   L Harper, 'Parihaka plea gains momentum'.

Of such postcolonial fantasists Ngai Tahu historian Jean Jackson summed up matters:

> 'Peaceful protest?' Never! Digging up roads and fencing of public highways is provocation. It disturbs the peace. And sadly, when 'someone' told Maori, or paid them anyway to create trouble, not only did it impede tribes' development in all ways, the next generations were held-back, bitterly complaining of muddy roads. Or no roads at all. One of the sad legacies muddling tribal politics, is earnest writers like Dick Scott or his supporters with a Mumble of Memberships in liberal unions, churches, schools or parties.[18]

18   Jean Jackson, op. cit.

Works Cited

(Refer also to the footnoted newspaper sources).

Behn, A. Oroonoko, or, The Royal Slave (London, 1688), online: http://ebooks.adelaide.edu.au/b/behn/aphra/b42o/

Belich, J. I Shall Not Die: Titokowaru's War 1868-69 (Wellington: Bridget Williams Books, 2010).

Bolton, K. R. 'The Politics of White Dispossession', Radix, No. 1, July 2012, National Policy Institute, Washington.

Brailsford, B. Song of the Waitaha: The Histories of a Nation (Christchurch: Ngatapuwae Trust, 1994).

Buchanan, R. The Parihaka Album: Lest We Forget (Wellington: Huia Books, 2010).

Bullert, G. 'Franz Boas as Citizen-Scientist: Gramscian-Marxist Influence on American Anthropology', The Journal of Social, Political and Economic Studies, Vol. 34, No. 2, Summer 2009.

Capper, R. 'One Woman's Battle for Recognition of Ngati Hotu', , Franklin E-Local, February 2011, http://www.elocal.co.nz/view_ Article~id~266~title~Listen_to_the_People._Talking_with_an_ Extinct_Race._Part_1.html

Clydesdale, G. 'Growing Pains: Evaluations and the Cost of Human Capital', Massey University, Palmerston North, New Zealand, 2008.

Courlander, H. The African (New York: Crown Publishers, 1967).

Davidson, B. Old Africa Rediscovered (London: Victor Gollancz, 1959).

Davidson, J. M. The Prehistory of New Zealand (Auckland: Longman Paul, 1984).

Doutré, M. Ancient Celtic New Zealand (Auckland: De Danann Publishers, 1999).

Doutré, M. The Littlewood Treaty – The True English Text of the Treaty of Waitangi – Found (Auckland: De Danann Publishers, 2005).

Emory University, 'Introduction to Postcolonial Studies', http://www. english.emory.edu/Bahri/Intro.html

Elkins, C. Imperial Reckoning: The Untold Story of Britain's Gulag in Africa (New York: Owl Books, 2005).

Encyclopedia of the Middle East, "Mahdi," http://www.mideastweb.org/Middle-East-Encyclopedia/mahdi.htm

Fell, B. 'Maoris from the Mediterranean', New Zealand Listener, 22 February, 1 March 1975.

Floyd, T. B. The Boer Nation's English Problem (Johannesburg, 1977).

Fogle, R W and S L Engerman, Time on the Cross: The Economics of American Slavery (Boston: Little Brown and Co., 1974).

Fraser, A. The WASP Question (London: Arktos Media Ltd., 2011), http://www.arktos.com/andrew-fraser-the-wasp-question.html

Fraser, A. 'the Cult of "The Other" and the End of Academic Freedom', Alterative Right, 2 March 2012, http://www.alternativeright.com/main/the-magazine/the-cult-of-the-other/

Freeman, D. Margaret Mead and Samoa: The Making and Unmaking of an Anthropological Myth (Harmondsworth, Middlesex: Penguin Books, 1984).

Gadd, B. 'The Teachings of Te Whiti O Rongomai 1831-1907, The Journal of the Polynesian Society, Vol. 75, No. 4, 1966.

Garden, D. S. Australia, New Zealand and the Pacific: An Environmental History (Santa Barbara: ABC-CLIO, 2005).

Gerhart, G. M. and C. L. Glaser. A Documentary History of African Politics in South Africa 1882-1990, Vol. 6, "From Protest to Challenge" (Bloomington: Indiana University Press, 2010).

Govett-Brewster Art Gallery, 'Colin McCahon: Parihaka Triptych 1972, Acrylic on canvass', http://www.govettbrewster.com/Exhibitions/ColinMcCahon.aspx

Haley, A. Roots: The Saga of an American Family (New York: Doubleday Books, 1976).

Hall, J. Memorandum to his Excellency from John Hall, Enclosure No. 1, Despatch No. 38, (No. 11) Government House, Wellington, New Zealand, 22 December, 1880; Appendices to the Journal of the House of Representatives, A1, 1881.

Harper, L. 'Parihaka plea gains momentum', Taranaki Daily News, 21 June 2012, http://www.stuff.co.nz/taranaki-daily-news/news/7142489/Parihaka-Day-plea-gains-momentum

Howe, K. R. The Quest for Origins: Who First Discovered and Settled

Works Cited

New Zealand and the Pacific Islands? (Penguin Books, 2003).

Human Rights Commission, 'Parihaka Management Trust', http://www.hrc.co.nz/race-relations/te-ngira-the-nz-diversity-action-programme/participants-2010/parihaka-management-trust/ <Accessed January 31, 2011).

Ihimaera, W. The Parihaka Woman (New York: Random House, 2011).

Jackson, J. 'A Strange Parihaka Bubble: Part of Taranaki's Saga', unpublished MS, Auckland, n.d.

Jones, J. 'Suicide Tape Transcript'; Mary McCormick Maaga, Hearing the Voices of Jonestown (Syracuse: Syracuse University Press, 1998), http://employees.oneonta.edu/downinll/mass_suicide.htm

King, M. L. 'Letter from a Birmingham Jail', 16 April 1963, African Studies Center, University of Pennsylvania, http://www.africa.upenn.edu/Articles_Gen/Letter_Birmingham.html

Landau, M., et al. Captive Hearts, Captive Minds (Alameda, California: Hunter House, 1994).

Leigh, R. L. Vereeniging History, (Town Council of Vereeniging, 1968), http://www.vaaltriangleinfo.co.za/history/vereeniging/index.htm

Mair, Capt. G. Kaingaroa, 'Its Passing to the Crown in 1879', Auckland Star Supplement, 1923, www.onenzfoundation.co.nz/KAINGAROA%20-%20ITS%20PASSING%20TO%20THE%20CROWN.doc

Maori Dictionary, http://www.maoridictionary.co.nz/

'Massey's Pasifika Director says report fails to recognise wider contribution of Pacific people', Massey University, Palmerston North, 27 May 2008, http://www.massey.ac.nz/massey/about-massey/news/article.cfm?mnarticle_uuid=27DC5253-96BF-57FE-AA70-353740D50ADE

Masson, S. 'Remembering the Vendée', http://www.lewrockwell.com/orig5/masson1.html

'Mau Mau Oaths', Candour, 22 July 1960, http://www.candour.org.uk/9-mau-mau-oaths/4550760289

'Mau Mau Trio Travel to High Court in Fight for Apology over claims they were Tortured', Daily Mail, 17 July 2012, http://www.dailymail.co.uk/news/article-2174640/Mau-Mau-trio-travel-High-Court-fight-apology-claims-tortured.html

McFadgen, B. 'Impact on the Landscape', J Wilson (ed.) From the

Beginning: The Archaeology of the Maori, (Auckland: Penguin Books, 1987).

McMaster, N. 'Te Whiti and the Parihaka Incident', 1945, unpublished thesis.

Mead, M. (1928) The Coming of Age in Samoa: A Psychological Study of Primitive Youth for Western Civilisation (New York: American Museum of Natural History 1973).

Medvedev, Z. A. The Rise and Fall of T D Lysenko (New York: Anchor Books, 1971).

Mitchell, A. A Fragile Paradise: Nature and Man in the Pacific (London: Collins, 1989).

New Zealand Historic Places Trust, 'Dunedin Prison (Former), Heroically Narrative: Maori', http://historic.org.nz/TheRegister/RegisterSearch/RegisterResults.aspx?RID=4035&m=advanced

Ngata, Sir A.The Treaty of Waitangi: An Explanation (Te Tiriti O Waitangi: He Wkakamarama) (Maori Purposes Fund Board, 1922).

Packenham, T. The Boer War (New York: Random House, 1979).

'Parihaka Past and Present. The Mecca of the Maori', *Grey River Argus*, 27 March 1911.

Parris, R. to Undersecretary for Native Dept., New Plymouth, May 15, 1882, Appendices to the Journal of the House of Representatives.

Pulitzer Prizes: 2006, General Non-Fiction, http://www.pulitzer.org/citation/2006-General-Nonfiction

Ranford, J. 'Pakeha, Its Origin and Meaning', http://maorinews.com/writings/papers/other/pakeha.htm

Riseborough, H. "A New Kind of Resistance;" K Day (ed.) Contested Ground: The Taranaki Wars 1860-1881 (Wellington: Huia Publications, 2010).

Roberts, Lt. Col. J. M. Armed Constabulary District Office, Opunake, Telegram to Under-Secretary, Native Office, Taranaki, 'Report of Native Meeting at Parihaka in June, 1885'.

Round, D. Truth or Treaty? Commonsense Questions About the Treaty of Waitangi (Christchurch, New Zealand: Canterbury University Press, 1998).

Rousseau, J. J. Discourse on the Origin of the Inequality Among Men, 1754, http://www.constitution.org/jjr/ineq.htm

Rusden, G. W. (1883) Aureretanga: Groans of the Maoris (Christchurch:

Works Cited

Capper Press, 1975).

Schoeder, R. Cults: Secret Sects and Radical Religions (London: Carlton Books, 2007).

Scott, R (Dick). Ask that Mountain: The Story of Parihaka (Auckland: Heinemann, 1975).

Sinclair, K. Kinds of Peace: The Maori People After the Wars 1870-85 (Auckland University Press, 1991).

'Slavery in Colonial Times', The Prow, http://www.theprow.org.nz/slavery-in-colonial-times/#.UBMWgaDYG24

Tacitus, Germania, http://www.fordham.edu/halsall/source/tacitus1.html

'Tatarakihi: The Children of Parihaka', http://www.nzff.co.nz/film/tatarakihi

Terrorist Watch, 'Mandela and the Church Street Bombing', http://www.netcomuk.co.uk/~springbk/enemy.html

The Taranaki Report: Kaupapa Tuatahi, (Wellington: Waitangi Tribunal, 1997).

U.S. Marshal's Service, "Incident at Wounded Knee," http://www.usmarshals.gov/history/wounded-knee/index.html

Utley, R. M. The Last Days of the Sioux Nation (New Haven: Yale University Press, 1963).

'Verwoerd Gives Riot Details, The Cape Times, 22 March 1960.

Weiser, K. 'Legends of America: The Ghost Dance: a Promise of Fulfilment', http://www.legendsofamerica.com/na-ghostdance.html

Wells, B. The History of Taranaki (New Plymouth: Edmondson & Avery, 1878).

Wheelers, The Parihaka Woman, 'Description', http://www.wheelers.co.nz/books/9781869797294-parihaka-woman-the/#desc

Why We Are White Refugees, 'The Road to Sharpeville and the ANC's Orwellian Memoryhole', http://why-we-are-white-refugees.blogspot.com/2010/03/road-to-sharpeville-and-ancs-orwellian.html

Winder, V. 'Pacifist of Parihaka – Te Whiti o Rongomai', Puke Ariki, New Plymouth District Council, 27 May 2003, http://www.pukeariki.com/Research/TaranakiStories/TaranakiStory/id/334/title/pacifist-of-parihaka-te-whiti-o-rongomai.aspx

Windshuttle, K. The Fabrication of Australian History (Sydney: Macleay Press, 2002).

Windshuttle, K. 'Postmodernism and the Fabrication of Aboriginal History', Lecture to New South Wales Higher School Certificate History Extension Conference, Sydney, May 30 2007, http://sydneyline.com/Postmodernism%20and%20Fabrication.htm

About The Author

K R Bolton has doctorates in theology and related areas, diplomas in psychology and social work studies, and Ph.D. honoris causa. He is a Fellow of the Academy of Social and Political Research (Athens), a 'contributing writer' for Foreign Policy Journal and has been widely published in both the scholarly and popular media. His other books include Revolution from Above (London: Arktos Media Ltd., 2011) and Artists of the Right (San Francisco: Counter-Currents Publishing, 2012). He has been translated into Vietnamese, Russian, French, German, Farsi, Italian, Latvian, Czech.

Other Books by Kerry Bolton include:

Revolution from Above
(London: Arktos Media Ltd., 2011)

The Psychotic Left
(London: Black House Publishing, 2013)

Babel Inc.,
(London: Black House Publishing, 2013)

Artists of the Right
(San Francisco: Counter-Current Publishing, 2012)

Stalin: The Enduring Legacy
(Black House Publishing 2012)

Peron and Peronism
(Black House Publishing 2014)

www.ingramcontent.com/pod-product-compliance
Lightning Source LLC
Chambersburg PA
CBHW070925270326
41927CB00011B/2730